The Birthing of a Kingdom Nation

Why God Wants His Church to Function as a Nation

ABRAHAM JOHN

The Birthing of a Kingdom Nation

Why God wants His church to function as a nation
Discipling Nations Series # 9

Copyright © 2023 by Abraham John

Published by Abraham John

www.Regnoethnos.com
email: mim@maximpact.org
1-800-558-5020
(720)-560-4664

ISBN: 978-1-948330-11-4

Published in the United States of America

Unless otherwise indicated, all Scripture is taken from the New King James Version®. Copyright © 1982 by omas Nelson.

Used by permission. Scripture marked (KJV) is from the King James Version of the Bible, which is in the public domain. Scripture marked (NLT) i s from New Living Translation, copyright © 1996, 2004, 2015 by Tyndale House Foundation. All rights reserved. Scripture marked (TLV) is from Tree of Life Translation of the Bible. Copyright © 2015 by the Messianic Jewish Family Bible Society.

All emphases or additions in parentheses within scriptural quotations are the author's own.

All rights reserved. No part of this book may be reproduced or transmitted in any form or by any means, electronic or mechanical, including photocopying, recording, or by any information storage and retrieval system, without permission in writing from the author. Please direct your inquiries to mim@maximpact.org

This book is dedicated to our heavenly Father, whose dream is to see all the nations worshipping Him. It's my dream to see at least one nation serving Him.

Contents

Preface	7
Introduction	11
Chapter 1: Why a Kingdom Nation?	23
Chapter 2: God's Purpose and Pattern	33
Chapter 3: God's Heart for the Nations	53
Chapter 4: God's Prototypes	59
Chapter 5: The Process of Becoming a Kingdom Nation—Part 1	83
Chapter 6: The Process of Becoming a Kingdom Nation—Part 2	101
Chapter 7: Discovering the Lost Father	121
Chapter 8: The Government of God - Part 1	151
Chapter 9: The Government of God - Part 2	167
Chapter 10: The Twelve Components of a Kingdom Nation	197
More Books & Resources	227

Preface

From 2023 onward, there is a major shift coming to this earth. The next seven years are going to be very critical for the body of Christ (2023-2029). That's why the Lord told me to release this book on January 1st of 2023. Things are going to get way out of control. We know that nothing has been the same since 9/11. Then the Covid Pandemic came, and nothing has been normal since. What the kingdom of darkness is about to unleash on the earth, and on humans, is like nothing we have ever seen before. The enemy knows his time is short, and something cataclysmic is going to happen to our planet.

With the release of this book, a major shift is going to happen on the earth. After I wrote this preface, Florida was hit by the worst storm in the last five hundred years. Nothing is going back to normal again. We will either prepare for it or fall victim to it. Every year, God gives me a word for that year. The word He gave me for 2020 was "get ready for change." To be honest with you, that's the year the Lord released me to do His kingdom assignment. Then, for 2021- 2022, it was the word "transition," and it referred to transitioning from religion into the kingdom.

The years 2020-2022 have been the most blessed and fruitful years of my life and ministry. If we prepare in advance, every crisis in the natural is an opportunity in disguise. It is time to prepare for what is coming, just like Joseph did in Egypt before the famine.

> "For behold, the day is coming,
> Burning like an oven,
> And all the proud, yes, all who do wickedly will be stubble.
> And the day which is coming shall burn them up,"
> Says the LORD of hosts,
> "That will leave them neither root nor branch.
> But to you who fear My name
> The Sun of Righteousness shall arise
> With healing in His wing;
> And you shall go out
> And grow fat like stall-fed calves. (Malachi 4:1-2)

God always warns and prepares His people for what is coming. The flood during Noah's time, the famine in Egypt, and Jesus's prediction about the destruction of the temple are some examples of how God told His people to prepare ahead of time.

The word God gave me for 2023 is "cataclysmic shift." The only other time I can compare to the darkness in this generation is the time of Noah. But He always prepares an "ark" for His people. There is only one force that can withstand and oppose what the kingdom of darkness is about to unleash. Only the kingdom of light (Kingdom Nation) can defeat the kingdom of darkness. This book is to prepare the body of Christ for what is coming.

Unfortunately, the church has been operating without the kingdom of God. The church believes that if they just keep doing what they have been doing for the past five hundred years, things are going to get better. Things have not gotten better. Though we have increased in number, we remain more divided and helpless than ever. More churches are closing

PREFACE

their doors than new ones opening. We have advanced technologically, but in morality, spirituality, family life, and loving one another, we score an all-time low.

We are in the midst of another industrial, economic, technological, political, social, and religious revolution. How do we prepare for what is coming? This book is the blueprint the Lord is releasing to His people for what we must do now. This book is about *reformation*, not *revival*. If we do not reform the way we operate, and adopt the kingdom way of doing things, then there is no hope left for us.

When Covid hit, most of God's people were unprepared. They did not know what to do. They had the *faith,* but there was no *work* to sustain them and bring them through the crisis. As a result, we lost many lives, businesses, and churches. Don't let that happen to you the next time around. The only way to be safe and secure is to be a part of what God is birthing on the earth now. Welcome to being a part of **The Birthing of a Kingdom Nation**.

Introduction

Hijacked Destiny

> And you shall love the Lord your God with all your heart, with all your soul, with all your mind, and with all your strength. This *is* the first commandment. (Mark 12:30)

Ever since the passing of Queen Elizabeth II, nations that have been part of the Commonwealth are talking about parting ways with the colonial era and the oppression it brought upon those nations. They want the sovereignty of their nations back. But the real question is, how many of us are free to serve and love the Lord our Creator with all of our heart, soul, mind, and strength?

How many of us have the freedom to obey the first and most important commandment in the Bible? It doesn't say that we may love the Lord, or to try to love Him the best we can. It says, "You shall." It's a commandment, or an order from the King. From the beginning of our lives till our last breath, we were created by God to love and serve Him only.

This commandment is applicable to every single believer, not just ministers. Do you know that God sent you to this earth to be a part of building His kingdom? Your entire life is supposed to be spent doing what He wants you to do—not just when you retire or for a few hours on the weekend.

God did not say to love Him with ten percent of our heart, soul, mind, and strength, or with what is left over after we have done everything we want to do. Or to love Him after loving everything and everyone else. No, He wants to be our first and foremost love. He wants to be our number one priority. He wants all of it—all of us—all of our heart, soul, mind, and strength.

Something happened to humanity. Something happened to this planet earth. Each one of us was created by God and sent to this earth to fulfill a very specific assignment for Him and for His kingdom. Each one of us plays an integral role in fulfilling the dream the Father has for the earth.

Why are the earth and this world in the shape they are in today? Whose fault is it that nothing is working the way it is supposed to work? It is because only a few of its inhabitants are free to do what they were created to do. Everyone else has been taken into slavery and is serving another king and kingdom. The majority have been trained by the Babylonian system to serve a master called money or mammon.

We were kidnapped, and our destiny has been hijacked. The reason we are not feeling like we have been kidnapped or taken captive is because for generations we have been programmed to function in a certain way, and we think that what we are doing, and the way we are living life, is normal because everybody else is doing the same thing.

The life we are living is not normal and should not be normal for us. What we see around us is not normal. This world shouldn't be this way. Something tragic happened to it. Our DNA has been mutated by the wrong religious beliefs and by what our forefathers went through in their lives. The DNA we inherited from our parents has been defective and mutated for generations.

INTRODUCTION

Why are Christians the least productive people in every country? We claim to serve a living and amazing and powerful God, but people who worship idols and demons seem to be more innovative, productive, and creative. Why? Why do people with Jesus in their heart feel hopeless and bound?

No Time for the Kingdom

One of our ministry partners shared her experience in the corporate world. She worked for a bank and dreaded waking up every morning, because when she woke up, she had to go to the office and a job she hated. The fact of waking up every morning to go to work and do something she hated disheartened and discouraged her. She didn't have a choice; she had three little children to feed and take care of, and what her husband earned was not enough to cover the household expenses.

She was forced to be a working mother and wife. She had to wake up at four o'clock in the morning to prepare food for the family; and then she had to wake up each child according to their age. The oldest one had to go to kindergarten, and then she prepared the other two to be dropped off at day care on the way to her office.

After work, she had to stop and pick up the kids from day care, come home and cook their dinner, wash clothes, tidy the house, and then get to bed late at night. She averaged only three or four hours of sleep and repeated the routine the next day. Her husband came home only once a week because of where he had to work.

She never had time for anything—no time to take care of herself or do anything that she enjoyed, and her health began to deteriorate. Life was dreadful, and waking up each morning to do something she hated killed any fulfillment or joy. She was not doing anything illegal or immoral; she was working for a bank at that time. If she didn't go to work, there would be no money for the family to survive.

THE BIRTHING OF A KINGDOM NATION

In her heart, she knew she was created to do something different. Though she was a believer and grew up in a Christian home, what she did not know was that she was sent by God to this planet to accomplish something specific for His kingdom. Though she wanted to serve God, she did not know how her family's needs would be met if she left her job and entered into what God created her to do. She was forced to give her strength, skill, and time to build a business, unaware that she was being used to build the kingdom of darkness. She was not building God's kingdom.

You might say that she was giving ten percent of her income to the church as a tithe. What we don't realize is what happens to the ninety percent that is left. Much of that ninety percent goes back into the kingdom of darkness to further its agenda on the earth. Even the ten percent we give to the church eventually ends up back in the hands of the unbeliever. In a nutshell, the majority of our strength, time, money, and skill are being used to build and fortify the kingdom of darkness, while they should be used to serve the Lord. This must change.

This is the story of untold millions who are suffering in silence. They feel frustrated, but they don't know what to do or who to talk to about it. They feel stuck in this rat race they call life and don't know what else there is other than what they already know and have been doing. No one told them about their purpose. The religious system they belong to has failed them miserably.

The religious system this precious woman was a part of tried to steal from the little money she had. They promised her health and wealth if she kept on giving; promising that, one day, the windows of heaven would be opened, and she would receive her breakthrough. Though she gave out of her lack, it seemed like nothing was happening, and her situation went from bad to worse.

INTRODUCTION

You might know someone who is stuck in a similar situation like the one described above. These people are being forced to do something they don't like; they are stuck in modern-day slavery. This is the story of believers and unbelievers alike. How can a believer love the Lord with all their heart, soul, mind, and strength when they are forced to do a job for survival six days a week?

The good news about this partner is that she discovered her kingdom assignment and left her *job.* She was then launched into the *work* that God had prepared for her before the foundation of the world (Ephesians 2:10). She has written many books and travelled to several countries, and is currently being mightily used by God around the world. She found her place in the kingdom of God.

You might think that not having enough money is our problem. It isn't. Here is the testimony of a twenty-seven- year-old young man who was working at a famous financial firm in Wallstreet in New York. He said he was making more money than he knew how to spend. He was happily married and was looking forward to their first child, but he felt miserable inside.

He couldn't figure out why he felt miserable, even though in the natural everything was going well for him. It took him some time to figure out the reason. He even wished he didn't make that much money. Finally, he figured out the reason for his misery—he was doing a soulless job that he didn't believe in.

The Nations Are Collapsing

Recently, I stayed at a global brand hotel in the U.S. for a few days. Usually, such hotels provide breakfast for their guests. One Monday morning, I went downstairs expecting to have a good breakfast, only to hear that there would be no breakfast that day. I was surprised. The manager told me that the chef took leave that day because he had been working seven days a week for five weeks straight.

I was amazed. How can an individual work seven days a week for five weeks nonstop? It's hard to imagine. But it's not unusual for people working in the hospitality industry, especially now. Whether they like it or not, they have to show up for work. Otherwise, they will get fired, which would make their situation even worse. Businesses all over the U.S. are struggling to find people to work.

I visit South Africa often to minister. It is one of my favorite countries in the world. But when I heard that South Africa has a forty-nine percent unemployment rate, my heart sank. I couldn't believe what I was hearing. Then I learned that the unemployment rate among the youth is even higher—sixty-nine percent. South Africa is one of the most developed countries in Africa, and it is rich with natural resources and human potential. Their current situation shows a total failure of the educational, political, and religious systems.

I recently read a news article about what is happening in the country of Afghanistan. Their economy collapsed, and people have no food to eat. Parents are forced to sell their children to buy a morsel of bread. They are selling body parts, like the kidneys of their children, for a few dollars so they can buy food. Friends, these are not horror stories from centuries ago; these are real atrocities that are happening in the world we are living in now.

Another country, Sri Lanka, is also going through a terrible time. Their economy collapsed, and people cannot find basic things they need to survive. The long lines at petrol (gas) stations are unreal. Finally, their president escaped to a foreign country in a military jet. He didn't know what to do to keep his country going. People came out to the streets

INTRODUCTION

protesting and rioting. They even ransacked the president's house. The government of that country completely failed its citizens.

Other countries are facing similar situations. Zimbabwe, Ukraine, Iran, and many countries on the South American continent have been going through economic and political crises for many years. Inflation and recession are the talk of the day. Is there a solution to these problems our world is facing?

Church people have the same old answer. They will say things like, "These are the signs of the end times," or, "The greatest revival is around the corner." Every time something goes wrong with this world system, preachers will say that it's the sign of Jesus's second coming. When something new happens in the fields of the economy and technology, preachers will jump up and down and condemn it, saying it's the mark of the beast.

I recently read in another Christian news article that cryptocurrency is the *new* mark of the beast. Two years ago, it was the vaccine that was said to be the mark of the beast. A few decades ago, it was the computer or the television that were described as the mark of the beast or the Antichrist.

We have seen many antichrists come and go in our lifetime. Many "prophesied" that the pope or some liberal American presidents were the Antichrist. They have come and gone, and the world is still here—with us in it. Any time we hear about wars or rumors of wars, preachers will come out with a new end-time theory and say the rapture is at hand. The truth is that anything that opposes Christ and His kingdom is the spirit of antichrist. This spirit has been in operation since the beginning of time.

One thing I don't understand is why Christians are more excited about words that are not mentioned even once in the Bible, like revival, rapture, leadership, trinity, crusade, church planting, etc., but very few have any interest in hearing about the message Jesus preached and taught the most while He was on the earth, which is the kingdom of God.

Recently, the presidents of Russia, Iran, and Turkey met and made a pact to work together. All the end-time prophets got a kick out of it. They started to post on social media that the world is going to end soon.

Modern-Day Slavery

Do you know how many people are currently in slavery around the world? The International Labor Organization (ILO) estimates suggest that fifty million people—or one out of every 150 people alive—are trapped in forced labor or forced marriages. That is up nearly ten million in number from just five years ago.

How many children that you know of dread getting up in the morning to go to school. If learning new things was fun and fulfilling, they would be happy to get up and go to school. As parents, we all went through that season with our children. Many parents are afraid to send their children to school now because they fear they may not come back alive due to the number of shootings that have occurred.

A bishop that I know told me he did everything that religion and the church offer but felt completely empty inside. He had to perform and pretend to be spiritual and holy because he was a leader of many. Then he discovered the message of the kingdom at the age of seventy, and he was totally transformed by it. He felt he was finally *home*. He found the answers that he had been looking for all his life.

The modern education system is nothing but a slave-breeding incubator. That's the purpose for which it was launched. Modern education

INTRODUCTION

institutions are there to raise up people to serve another king and his kingdom. That's where slaves are being raised up and conditioned to go and do a job for the next thirty to forty years—often something they do not enjoy and won't bring any fulfillment to them.

There are exceptions. There is always that one student who was the best and excelled in school. Do you remember that student in your class? There was one in my class also. They love to study; they excel in every subject. They are the teacher's pet. But the majority are not born to excel in such an environment.

I am not against education; however, Jesus did not say to seek first a good education and then a secure job. He told us to seek first His kingdom and His righteousness. Once we seek and find His kingdom, and our assignment in it, fulfilling that assignment will require a specific type of education—then we should go for it.

What is the purpose of education? We have been programmed to think that the purpose of education is to prepare a person to get a job that pays well. That is not the purpose of education in God's kingdom. The ultimate purpose of Kingdom Education is to equip a person to establish God's kingdom and will on earth.

This is only achieved through helping individuals discover their God-given purpose. Training is then necessary to enable them to fulfill that purpose. The process for this is recognizing what they are called to do, and developing their potential and the gifts and talents God gave them, in order to establish their identity as sons and daughters of God—reconnecting them to their heavenly Father through Jesus Christ. If the education we received has not helped us achieve the above-mentioned goals, then we did not receive the right kind of education. Instead, we were raised up to become slaves to a system.

An Opportunity in the Chaos

The systems of this world will continue to collapse. When that happens, it is an opportunity for God's people to let their light shine brighter. But there is a problem with the children of God right now. They don't know what to do. They have neither the keys nor the resources to address the issues they are facing in the world around them. Their mindsets have been programmed by religion.

The sad reality is that the majority of the people on earth live and die without ever discovering why they were born. It is the same in the church. By the time many discover why they were born, it is too late for them. Don't let that happen to you or your children.

I am not trying to scare you with this information. In fact, this book is about the greatest news you will hear in this generation. The purpose of this book is to provide the solution the church and the world are looking for. This is not a book about revival as we know it. But, if you read and apply what is written, your spirit will be revived, and the eyes of your understanding will be enlightened (Ephesians 1:18). You will begin to see the church and the world from a new perspective, and your life will never be the same again.

The reason the church is not effective today is not because we don't have the Holy Spirit or the gifts of the Spirit. The Holy Spirit never left the church or the planet. The reason the church cannot offer any solution to the problems our world is facing isn't because we don't have enough buildings and facilities. The reason we are not effective is because we missed God's blueprint—we lost our purpose. This book is about rediscovering that blueprint.

This is also a prophetic book about the future of the church and how to prepare the body of Christ to become everything God ordained for

INTRODUCTION

us and go where God wants to take us. Otherwise, the chance is that the church will go through another dark age. This book is not about the end time as we think of it, but the end of an era and the beginning of a new one. The religious church system we knew came to an end many years ago.

If we do not heed the voice of the Lord and make the changes now, many lives will be lost as a result, and the earth will have to go through another five-hundred-year cycle while waiting for the next season. In that case, we won't be here, so we must hope the next generation will capture the vision and the road map provided by God in this book and run with it. This is not a normal book that you will read. This is a "scroll from heaven." It contains the heart of God for the church and the nations of the earth. Welcome to the birthing of a Kingdom Nation.

Chapter 1

Why a Kingdom Nation?

Now it shall come to pass in the latter days That the mountain of the LORD's house shall be established on the top of the mountains, and shall be exalted above the hills; and all nations shall flow to it. (Isaiah 2:2)

Life on earth started in a garden (Genesis 2:8), and it ends with a city inside a garden. That city is called the bride of Christ (Revelation 21:9-10). How can a city be called a bride? You will find the answer in this book.

What is God doing on the earth today? Many are asking this question. They are looking in the wrong places and missing what He is doing—they can't see the forest for the trees. Every move of God since the beginning of time was sent to accomplish one single purpose, which is to establish His kingdom on the earth. When we miss His purpose, and use it to build an organization or a denomination, that particular move of God will come to an end.

In our prayer meetings, we tell God what to do, where to move, and how to move. We are trying to put God Almighty into a religious box and a paradigm that we have become used to. Every time we try to do that, we miss God because He doesn't fit into any man-made structure or system or religion.

That's how the Jewish leaders in the first century missed their Messiah. God was walking among them, doing things no man could do, but they still questioned and rejected Him because He did not fit into their religious paradigm. He did not do things the way they thought or wanted. So they decided He could not be God or from God. They misjudged Him and said that what was happening was not of God but of the devil. So they rejected Him and missed their season and destiny.

I believe the same thing is happening today. We are missing God and what He is doing in our midst because we are so fixated on how He should move and how we think He should do things. One of the greatest tragedies in life is to miss God when He finally answers the cry of our hearts that we have been crying for centuries. At the same time, the greatest thing we can do is to partner with God in what He is doing—in total surrender to Him and to His will.

From Rituals to Relationship

God made life very simple for us; religion always makes things difficult and impossible. Religion makes what has been made accessible to us so distant and what has been given to us freely by God very costly. It makes God's blessings and approval seem unattainable.

Religion won't allow us to know God; it only lets us talk *about* Him and know *about* Him, but not know Him. It keeps us talking about what happened in the past and what is going to happen in the future, with nothing for the present.

Religion separates us from God and alienates us from His purpose and plans. We become mere creatures of habit and ritual. Then we try to fit God within the framework of those habits and rituals. Every time God speaks or does something outside of the religious tradition we are used to, we reject and fight against it saying it can't be God. Every time we do that, we miss God and His move.

Then we quote a Bible verse to justify our ways and to secure our man-made traditions. If quoting Bible verses was considered a sign of spiritual maturity, Satan would be considered the most spiritual and mature; he also quotes scriptures—even to God Himself.

The sign of spiritual maturity is not defined by the number of verses we can quote or by how long we have been doing something a certain way inside a building we call a church, but it is defined by the ability to sense and discern what the Holy Spirit is speaking and doing *now* . We must have the courage and flexibility to make necessary changes to the way we think and operate, and to make room for God to do what He wants to do. We must have the capacity to adopt new systems and methods to sustain and grow what He started, so we can become the solution to the problems our world is facing. The church is called to stay ahead of the world, not lag behind and follow it.

Every ritual and habit produces certain emotions in humans, especially when it involves certain types of music or if our body is involved. Sometimes we interpret these emotions as God, or from Him, as if He is creating them. The good news is that God never changes, but our emotions and moods change at any given moment. We must surrender our emotions to God so we won't be distracted by them. God is always moving, and we must be free to trust and follow where He leads.

Why do we keep doing what we are doing? How long are we going to continue to do it? Are we doing it because of our religious traditions, or is it because the Holy Spirit is telling us to do it? If we examine our life, we will find that the majority of the things we do in church and in our lives are because of mere tradition or because they are things that keep us in our comfort zone and give us a false sense of security and control.

If we look at the church world today, how did we end up the way we are? How did all of these denominations and organizations come about? Did Jesus tell us to go and "plant" churches on every nook and corner? We have more churches on the planet than at any other time, but the world is more lost than ever.

Where in the Bible do we read that when we play slow music or songs it is called worship? Did Jesus or the apostles ever ask anyone if they want to go to heaven after they die? I couldn't find a single reference to any of the above-mentioned *doctrines* we hold so dear to our hearts.

We have not been willing to be honest with ourselves and ask some simple questions. We have not been willing to address them because they are considered "holy cows" of our belief system and have been in practice for years. We must be willing to admit our religiosity and to change.

The majority of people today feel isolated and lonely. They do not receive the support and encouragement they need. Nobody can fulfill their assignment on their own. We need each other, and that is why we are called a body, not an instrument or a tool. So they remain spiritually barren, socially isolated, and mentally unproductive. Though there are billions of people on the earth, there are more lonely people than at any other time. They are not yet a part of this Kingdom Nation and tribe. We welcome you to join God's family and become a part of what He is doing on the earth today.

What is a Nation?

A nation is a group of people, families, clans, and tribes with a common goal, and a common vision, language, and culture.

A Kingdom Nation is not a ministry, network, or organization. It is a nation whose King is Jesus Christ. It is a global nation made of people from every individual nation and tongue. My dream is for Him to have at least one nation on earth that serves Him with everything they have. The great commission is about discipling nations, but we haven't been able to disciple even a single nation yet. The reason is simple; before we are able to disciple other nations with the gospel of the kingdom, the body of Christ must first become a Kingdom Nation.

Only a nation can disciple another nation, just like only an individual can disciple another individual. Only a kingdom can colonize another kingdom. That is how colonialization started. That is what God is doing on the earth today. This is the LORD's doing; it is marvellous in our eyes. (Psalm 118:23, KJV)

The season of big crusades, mega churches, and superstars in the body of Christ is over. God is dismantling and removing every boundary and wall that man has built to separate and divide us. We must become one as Jesus prayed to the Father in John 17. The world is laughing at us because the salt has lost its flavor.

Crusades and individuals cannot disciple a nation. Powerful kingdoms went and colonized other nations and made them part of their kingdom. Though we do not use the same methods of those colonizers, the principle is the same. God has always wanted a nation to be the prototype for every other nation to copy and follow. The whole world is waiting and looking for solutions that only the church can offer them. They won't listen to us, or believe us, until we have the proof to show them.

The Mountain of the Lord

Once the mountain of the Lord that we read about in Isaiah 2:2, which is His kingdom and the Kingdom Nation, is set and established, all other nations will flow into it automatically. We do not need to use any tricks or false advertisements, or healing and miracles, to gather a crowd. It will be a natural response of the nations. They need what we have. Now the problem is that we do not have any proof to show. If we build it, they will come.

You don't take a precious commodity or a product of value and try to sell it from house to house, or on the roadside, and then beg people to buy it. If something is of value, and if you really need it, you will go looking for it. You will even travel to other countries to find it and pay for it.

You won't see anyone trying to sell gold from the side of the road or from a makeshift shop. If they do, nobody will go there to buy it because they will think it is fake. Gold is valuable, and people are willing to pay the price to own a piece of it. When you want to visit a city or a resort, they won't come to you, you need to go where they are. You might have heard about them through the news or an advertisement.

This is the way the kingdom of God and the mountain of God operate. The kingdom of God is the most precious treasure we have and that we can offer. Jesus compared His kingdom to a treasure hidden in a field. The reason people don't want it now, or don't appreciate it, is because they don't see or understand the value of it. Why do people from all over the world want to come to the United States? It is because they heard about its greatness and prosperity, and they want a piece of it. People will do any daring thing to reach this country.

When people get a revelation of the kingdom of God, they will come from all over the world to see and experience it. Believe me, this will happen and it must happen. Jesus did not go begging people to receive Him or to accept Him. Neither did He run around trying to save everyone to take them to heaven. His mission was not to populate heaven with humans; His mission was to bring heaven to earth.

WHY A KINGDOM NATION?

It was during David's time that the kingdom of God was established in Israel. It was the most prosperous kingdom on earth. David appointed his son Solomon as the next king. Solomon did not have to fight any battles because all the enemies had been defeated and brought to his footstool. The earth remained subdued under him.

> Is not the Lord your God with you? And has He *not* given you rest on every side? For He has given the inhabitants of the land into my hand, and the land is subdued before the Lord and before His people. (1 Chronicles 22:18)

> Then the fame of David went out into all lands, and the Lord brought the fear of him upon all nations. (1 Chronicles 14:17)

It was the most prosperous kingdom nation:

> Of gold and silver and bronze and iron *there is* no limit. Arise and begin working, and the Lord be with you. (1 Chronicles 22:16)

> All King Solomon's drinking vessels *were* gold, and all the vessels of the House of the Forest of Lebanon *were* pure gold. Not *one was* silver, for this was accounted as nothing in the days of Solomon. (1 Kings 10:21)

> The king made silver *as common* in Jerusalem as stones, and he made cedar trees as abundant as the sycamores which *are* in the lowland. (1 Kings 10:27)

Kings, queens, and people of fame from around the world came to Jerusalem to meet King Solomon and to hear his wisdom. All nations began to flow to Jerusalem to experience this kingdom nation. They heard about its glory even to the ends of the earth. When they came, they brought huge amounts of gold, silver, and other precious things as gifts to present to the king.

And men of all nations, from all the kings of the earth who had heard of his wisdom, came to hear the wisdom of Solomon. (1 Kings 4:34)

For he was wiser than all men—than Ethan the Ezrahite, and Heman, Chalcol, and Darda, the sons of Mahol; and his fame was in all the surrounding nations. (1 Kings 4:31)

This is a prophetic picture of what the Lord has always wanted. It is a pattern mentioned in the Bible for us to understand and follow. We do not need to go and beg people to believe in Jesus or to come to church. They should come to us and want to be a part of our lives. How will this happen?

When the famine happened in Egypt and other parts of the world, people came to Joseph to buy grain because they heard there was food in Egypt. That was because of Joseph and the wisdom he displayed to prepare for the famine. He did not have to go to witness for Jehovah. People came to him looking for a solution.

So all countries came to Joseph in Egypt to buy *grain*, because the famine was severe in all lands. (Genesis 41:57)

We see the same pattern in the Bible during Elijah and Elisha's time. People from other kingdoms came looking for them. God has always wanted His people to be the light of this world and salt of the earth. Esther, Mordecai, and Daniel are other examples. (Esther 9:4; Daniel 1:17 & 19; 2:48; 6:3)

Isaiah prophesied about this—how the mountain of the Lord and His house should function. When we become a kingdom nation, we will be the mountain of the Lord on the earth and all the nations will flow to us, looking for help. That is God's design and plan from the beginning. Now, we go to other nations looking for help and sometimes begging. It is a reproach to the name of our Lord and a shame to His kingdom.

You might ask, "Didn't Jesus tell us to go to the ends of the earth?" Yes, He did. Once we become a kingdom nation, we will send out ambassadors to every nation and sphere of life to declare the praise of our King and the glory of His kingdom. Only a nation can send out ambassadors to represent that nation and its government. This is the kingdom order. Until now, we have been doing things based on the training we received under the religious system. The way a kingdom operates is different than how a religion operates.

> Now it shall come to pass in the latter days *That* the mountain of the LORD's house Shall be established on the top of the mountains and shall be exalted above the hills; and all nations shall flow to it. (Isaiah 2:2)

> Now it shall come to pass in the latter days *That* the mountain of the LORD's house Shall be established on the top of the mountains and shall be exalted above the hills; and peoples shall flow to it. (Micah 4:1)

> Both of the above verses say the same thing, and it happened during the time of the New Testament. The fame of Jesus spread throughout the region, and people from around the nations came to see Him. (Matthew 4:24)

Jesus said, "The queen of the South will rise up in the judgment with this generation and condemn it, for she came from the ends of the earth to hear the wisdom of Solomon; and indeed a greater than Solomon *is* here." (Matthew 12:42)

Why would Jesus say that He is greater than Solomon? Solomon was the wisest man who ever lived. People from all over the world came to Jerusalem to hear his wisdom. But Jesus is greater than Solomon in every way.

Solomon received his wisdom from Jesus.

> In whom (Jesus) are hidden all the treasures of wisdom and knowledge. (Colossians 2:3)

When the Kingdom Nation is established, it will be the most blessed and glorious nation on planet earth. All the kings and great people will bring their riches and glory to that nation to honor the Lord.

> And the nations of those who are saved shall walk in its light, and the kings of the earth bring their glory and honor into it. (Revelation 21:24)

> And they shall bring the glory and the honor of the nations into it. (Revelation 21:26)

There are a lot of similarities between the reign and the kingdom of Solomon and the reign and the kingdom of Jesus Christ. Solomon is a type, or shadow, of Christ in the old covenant.

This book is about the process of how the body of Christ can become that nation. God is bringing believers from around the globe to be a part of this great move. We need to become the Lord's house set on a hill, so all nations can flow into the kingdom of God.

> Let the heavens rejoice, and let the earth be glad; and let them say among the nations, "The LORD reigns."
> (1 Chronicles 16:31)

Chapter 2

God's Purpose and Pattern

> Then God said, "Let there be light"; and there was light.
> (Genesis 1:3)

Light

God started by releasing the light in Genesis 1:3, which is His blueprint for planet earth and everything He ever wanted to be done, built, and created. Light, in the Bible, means blueprint, model, pattern, revelation, or master plan. By saying, "Let there be light," God released His master plan for the entire earth and the world.

Then God showed Adam how that master plan (blueprint) looks in the natural by planting a garden in Eden. He took Adam and put him in the garden to tend and to keep it. Adam's life was the model (blueprint) for the rest of mankind to follow. His responsibility was to expand the garden and fill the entire earth to make it look like the model God showed him in Eden.

If nothing manifests on the earth (physical realm), then all of our efforts are in vain. We can do all the talk and dancing, but if nothing changes on the earth for the better, it's all a waste of time.

Through disobedience, we lost the garden. But God's purpose and plan remain the same for the earth. Next, God revealed that plan to the nation of Israel and entrusted them with that blueprint. He told them to shine that light to the gentiles—to take His salvation to the ends of the earth (Isaiah 49:6).

They refused to do it and neglected God's plan and design, so God decided to call people from among the gentiles and entrusted them with that light and blueprint. Jesus told the religious leaders that the kingdom of God will be taken from them and given to another nation that bears the fruit of it. That nation is the church—I call it the Kingdom Nation.

That's why Jesus said we are the light of this world (Matthew 5:14). Jesus is the Light of this world. In Him was life, and the life was the light of men (John 1:4). The life we see in Jesus, and how He lived, should be the example, model, pattern, or blueprint for everyone to follow. That is why Jesus is called the Last Adam (1 Corinthians 15:45).

God's Challenge

God created this earth to establish His kingdom. He is a King, and it is a king's nature to expand his kingdom to new territories. The Bible says that in the beginning, God created the heavens and the earth. Heaven is spiritual and earth is physical. Heaven is invisible to the natural eyes, and earth is the visible realm. Earth is made of natural sub- stance, and heaven is made of spiritual or invisible matter that is both fluid and solid at the same time. It can be made visible or invisible at any given moment.

Heaven and earth are governed by laws that were established by God. God is Spirit, and He lives in heaven. Heaven is His throne. Earth is the physical or natural realm. If anyone needs to live and operate on

GOD'S PURPOSE AND PATTERN

the earth, they are required to have a physical or material body. God doesn't have a physical or material body like ours, but He created the earth to expand His kingdom.

It is illegal for any spirit without a physical body to operate on the earth. Something or someone that gives legal right to any spirit to operate in the earth realm is called a gate. Anything or anyone that would give God the legal right to operate on the earth is called a gate of heaven. Whatever gives the enemy the legal right to operate on the earth is called a gate of hell.

God's challenge is that He doesn't have a physical body to live, and accomplish His will, on the earth. He decided to come up with a solution. He decided to make a physical form from the earth and put His Spirit inside that form. He came down to earth and made a body from the materials of the earth. Then He breathed the breath of life into the nostrils of that form and called what He made "Adam" or "mankind."

Humans are spirit beings who have a physical body. Our spirit came from God. He created us that way so He can accomplish His purpose through us. With our spirit, we can connect with God and access heaven because our responsibility is to bring what is in heaven to earth—the invisible to the visible. Our mind and body are the places of transition, where things that are in the spirit realm can be made manifest into the visible. Our mind picks up and translates what is in our spirit and transfers it to our body so that what is in our spirit, and what we saw in the spirit, can be made manifest in the natural realm.

Our body was made to make what is invisible, visible. To make what is spiritual, natural. Whatever God wants to accomplish on the earth, He first deposits it into our spirit through His Spirit or through His Word. Then it gets translated through our mind, for our mind is the bridge between our spirit and body. What is in our mind or imagination then materializes in the natural through the "works" we do. That is why the Bible says we are His workmanship created in Christ Jesus for good works (Ephesians 2:10).

What is it that God wants to see done on the earth? Why did He create humans and put them on the earth? If He wanted all of us in heaven, He would have kept us all there in the first place. Why would He put us on the earth to suffer like this? Some would say that God put us here to teach and train us for the future: for eternity.

Heaven is a kingdom. That is why it is called the kingdom of heaven. Jesus told us to pray for His kingdom to come to earth and for His will to be done on earth as it is in heaven. God wants to bring His kingdom from heaven to earth. This can only be accomplished through humans. That is why He created us with dual citizenship of heaven and earth and as both natural and spiritual beings.

Our responsibility is to see what is happening in heaven and copy it on earth. God did a favor for us. He decided to establish a prototype nation on earth as an example for us to see, live, and experience. He came down and planted a garden in Eden. The garden of Eden was the first prototype kingdom nation God established on the earth. Our responsibility was to duplicate, expand, and make the entire earth look like the garden.

Jesus' Challenge

Jesus had a challenge. When He was sent to His people, they did not receive Him or the message He preached. They were more concerned with starting another synagogue in another town to propagate the new interpretation of the Law by a different Rabbi. They prided themselves on their religious traditions and their spiritual roots saying they were the seed of Abraham.

They missed God and His plan for them. They lost the kingdom of God and His assignment. Instead, they became a religious and political entity under the leadership of men that were appointed by people. Every time God's people missed His kingdom agenda, they succumbed to mere Jewish nationalism.

Nationalism is a cry for survival. It is the voice of the rejected and the misunderstood. Under the spirit of nation-alism, people will rally behind any crook who will promise them what their flesh is looking for. The majority of the time, it is their political freedom or preservation. That is why the Jewish leaders loved Barabbas, a murderer, more than Jesus, their King. Barabbas promised them a *political nation* without God's kingdom. They were looking for a Jewish nation, not a kingdom nation.

There are many today who are trying to establish Christian nations by enforcing Christian laws and by the might of a military or a political party. These are nothing but the repetition of failed attempts from our past. Either we learn from our history and become better, or we will keep repeating it.

How do we establish a kingdom nation without a Christian political party or without being part of one? A king-dom nation has nothing to do with any political parties of this world. This comes at a later stage. Jesus's kingdom doesn't operate like the kingdoms of this world. He did not come to start a righteous political party or a Jewish nation. I will explain more about this later in the book.

The Making of a Kingdom Nation

Though God walked among the people of Israel in human form, the religious people were always asking for a sign. The reason is because they only learned to connect with God on the basis of what benefits them or of power. We need to learn to connect with God not only on the basis of miracles but on the basis of our relationship with Him as our Father and King, in the context of His kingdom. Mankind has yet to learn to relate with God on the basis of His kingdom. Many people these days talk or use the word "kingdom," but what that really means to them is just miracles, souls, or revival.

The same thing happened to the people of Israel in the wilderness. They only knew God based on the miracles they saw, so they always looked for another one. They refused to know Him and His ways, and they perished in the wilderness.

In the beginning, it was not so. God did not create Adam to live by miracles. God did not introduce Himself to Adam as the Miracle Worker. Adam was the son of God, and God wanted him to relate with Him as his Father, in the context of His kingdom purpose on the earth. That's why He put him in the garden where there was no lack.

People will say that revival is happening in this country or that city, and then they will go to another place and have a revival for a few days. But they never come to the true knowledge of God as their Father, and they do not understand His purpose for mankind or the earth. They are tossed to and fro by every wind of doctrine, by the trickery of men (Ephesians 4:14).

The truth is that God is always moving. It's not that we are waiting for Him to do something; it is He who has been waiting for us to come to the knowledge of the truth. When we know the truth, it will bring us to freedom, not a temporary revival.

From the beginning of time, God has been in the business of making a kingdom nation that will function as a prototype for others to follow in order to manifest His kingdom on earth. That is why Jesus called the church a nation. That is why we never see a church service started in the Bible with three fast songs and two slow songs. It was a governing body coming together to execute the will of their King.

It is also why Jesus did not give us a program on how to conduct a church service. The Ekklesia is so fluid and flexible that it will fit into any culture or circumstance. We shouldn't be meeting all the time for the same reason and with the same program. Just like the governing body of a nation meets to address, solve, or legislate different issues or laws, we should be meeting the same way. The Bible never talks about a building when it talks about the Ekklesia because the Ekklesia is not limited to any type or style of building.

Flowing with God

Every nation is different from each other. Their languages, cultures, and foods are different. That is how the Ekklesia is supposed to operate, not with a written liturgy or program. It should be what the Holy Spirit wants to be done anywhere and at any given moment, and exactly the way He wants it to be done. A local Ekklesia should be ready to flow with Him in any covert or overt operation to overthrow the gates of hell and their assignments before they manifest in the natural.

It does not require three fast songs and two slow songs for God to manifest. God is not a *genie* that is locked up in a bottle. A genie won't manifest unless you say the exact mantra or do certain rituals exactly as they are required. Many treat God like they treat a genie. They believe He won't manifest until we strike that exact music note, and then He will show up.

First of all, what they don't understand is that the God they worship has been living inside them the entire time. He came into that building with them when they came in. Second, Jesus said that where two or three are gathered in His name, He will come and be in their midst (Matthew 18:20). But we don't recognize Him because we have been programmed differently by religion, and we miss Him the same way the first-century Jewish religious leaders missed Him.

They were still doing all of the religious rituals and sacrifices to please God and for His presence to show up while He was already walking among them in bodily form. He dwelt among them full of glory, truth, and grace, but they did not recognize Him.

The same things that happened to the nation of Israel happened to the church. During Jesus's time, synagogues were very popular. Instead of living as a nation and manifesting God's kingdom, the nation of Israel became divided into hundreds of pieces. There emerged many religious groups and sects based on different interpretations of the Scriptures. Why? Because they lost the purpose of God.

Rabbis and teachers came up with their own interpretation of the law, established a synagogue, and created a following after their own name. Then it grew and became a sect; we read about such sects and factions in the New Testament. Pharisees and Sadducees were the most popular ones.

One night, one of those religious leaders went to see Jesus privately. I believe this man felt a divine dissatisfaction in his spirit about what he was doing. His name was Nicodemus. What was Jesus's response to him? He brought him back to God's original idea or intent. He didn't tell him to recite the Torah five more times a day. He talked to him about the kingdom of God (John 3:1-5).

And that is exactly what happened to the church. The church is supposed to function as a nation and establish God's kingdom on earth. But because we lost our purpose, different preachers came up with their own interpretations of the Word. They created a following through their writings and established a Christian synagogue that we call the church.

We see them all across the nations and around the globe. Most of them are not fulfilling God's purpose for which He started the church—the Ekklesia.

By joining many of those synagogues together, they started denominations. The main focus of many of these leaders is to grow and expand their denominations by adding more synagogues and members to their religious system. Then they travel to other nations to recruit new members and to collect their tithes and offerings. The religious leaders during Jesus's time did exactly the same.

> Woe to you, scribes and Pharisees, hypocrites! For you travel land and sea to win one proselyte, and when he is won, you make him twice as much a son of hell as yourselves. (Matthew 23:15)

That is a serious crime. Those religious people made other people's lives twice as much a hell as theirs. We see so many such Christian synagogues that we call "church" all around us today. People are as lost as ever. They don't know why God put them on the earth. They don't know their purpose. They don't know what God thinks of them. And they don't know the heart of the Father. Their life is filled with hell, and they are waiting to escape to go to heaven. Lord, have mercy!

What a Kingdom Nation Looks Like

God is in the process of restoring and restarting this Kingdom Nation across the globe. He is rekindling His original idea, from the beginning, in the hearts and spirits of His children across the world. They are tired of the tyranny and slavery of this world system and religion. Their hearts and spirits are yearning for God's kingdom. They misunderstand that longing as the desire to go to heaven because of the misinformation they have received from religious sources.

Just like Jesus walked away from any man-made structures or temples, He already walked away from all the current religious structures and buildings that we call church. But they keep on doing the same old things thinking that one day God will show up in their midst and do something.

The Kingdom Nation is not like any other physical nation that we know of, and it does not have physical boundaries. This Kingdom Nation is going to function first within the physical nation in which we were born and live. It is made of believers who are born again and want to see God's kingdom and His will manifest on the earth. This starts just like Jesus said: the kingdom of heaven is like a mustard seed, a leaven, or yeast. It starts small, but it will grow until it takes over the whole earth.

We don't take over with spears and guns, and we don't protest or attempt a coup. Jesus did not protest against Rome or its emperors. That is not how His kingdom operates. Many religious zealots try to do what Barabbas and his followers did during Jesus's time. They protested against Rome, and he was arrested and put in prison. That is how the kingdoms of this world operate.

God's kingdom operates covertly, most of the time, but you can see and experience its fruit or result on the outside. That is how Joseph, Daniel, and Esther lived and made God's praises glorious in those nations and kingdoms. They did not walk around with a boom box, colored lights, and a music band. That is not how we are to make His praise glorious first.

We make God's praise glorious by manifesting His glory, His power, and His wisdom to the world by solving their problems, and to the principalities in the heavenly places. Most Christians are hesitant about their purpose. This is because they have been misinformed and were not taught about their purpose.

On Earth As it is in Heaven

When God created the earth, He created it to be an extension of His kingdom. He never intended for life on earth to be any different than life in heaven. He wanted earth to be like heaven. If something is not in heaven, it is illegal for it to exist on the earth. Everything that is in heaven has the potential to manifest on the earth.

Next, God created human beings. We are spirit beings who originated in God in eternity. His Spirit gave life to the body that was taken from the earth. With God's Spirit came the kingdom of God to dwell in us. God is King, and He has a kingdom. When His Spirit comes, His nature (image and likeness) also comes. Each one of us carries a "piece" of the kingdom within us. That is why Jesus said that the kingdom of God is within us (Luke 17:21). No human carries the entire kingdom within them. Our assignment is to manifest that piece of the kingdom that we carry on the earth.

In our spirit, we are one with God. We carry in our spirit the same essence He does. With our body, we relate to the earth. Both the earth and our body are physical. Our spirit is an unlimited material or substance, and our mind has the capacity to imagine. Through imagination, our mind captures what is in our spirit, from the spirit realm, and brings it into a virtual reality. That is how we conceive or perceive the will of God in our spirit. But we have not materialized it yet on the earth. As long as it is not manifested in the physical, it is not useful on the earth.

When we are born again, we are supposed to see the kingdom that is inside of us (John 3:3). We won't all see the same thing. Each one of us will see an aspect of God's kingdom that we were created to manifest on the earth. Each one of us carries a piece of the puzzle. When we put them all together, we will get the complete picture. When all humans created by God manifest the kingdom that is inside of them, this earth will be turned to heaven, and we will see God's will done on earth as it is in heaven.

What we see in the spirit (virtual reality) needs to be made manifest in the physical realm. It happens through the works we do. That is how we make earth like heaven. That is our true assignment.

When the Bible says, "on earth as it is in heaven," it means the real thing, or the blueprint. For everything that needs to manifest on the earth, there is an actual thing or place with the exact name in heaven. Everything God wants to manifest on the earth already exists in heaven. He communicates that through His Spirit to an individual who is committed to doing His will.

That is why the Bible says, "The eyes of the Lord run to and fro throughout the whole earth, to show Himself strong on behalf of those whose heart is loyal toward Him" (2 Chronicles 16:9). That means that He is looking for people who are willing to partner with Him in manifesting His will on earth as it is in heaven. Many times, He can't find the right individual.

There is nothing wrong with being heavenly minded, but if we are not manifesting what we see happening or existing in heaven, then we are no earthly good. Whatever has happened on the earth for God's purpose, we read that it already exists in heaven.

For everything God did on the earth, the original is in heaven. Do you know there is a Jerusalem in heaven and there is a Mount Zion in heaven? There is a tabernacle or temple in heaven. There is an Ekklesia or church in heaven (Hebrews 12:22). There are mountains in heaven (Revelation 21:10). When God called Moses to build the tabernacle, He told him to make sure to build it exactly as the one he was shown that exists in heaven. God gave the blueprint to Moses while he was on the mountain with God.

GOD'S PURPOSE AND PATTERN

> And see to it that you make *them* according to the pattern which was shown you on the mountain. (Exodus 25:40)

Moses had a spiritual experience with God on top of the mountain. When he came down, he instructed people to build the tabernacle as he saw it with God. That is what we should be doing with our life. That is what Jesus was doing while He was on the earth. And that is why He spent so much time in prayer.

Jesus was not telling the Father what to do or how and when to do something, but that is what most of our prayers have become. Most people spend their prayer time telling God what they want Him to do. There is nothing wrong with asking our Father for our needs, but if that is all we do, then we are missing so much of what prayer is supposed to be and also in our relationship with Him. He has so much to tell and show us—more than what we can ask or imagine. There is so much more than what God has already told us or written in His Word.

That is why Jesus told the disciples that He has so much more to tell them, but they were not ready to receive it (John 16:12). Though God has so much He wants to share with us, He will only tell us what we can bear, or handle.

Following the Blueprint

During prayer, Jesus was receiving a blueprint of everything He had to do that day. He received His daily schedule by meeting with His Father on a daily basis. Then He went out and did exactly what He saw. Jesus was not running around helping and saving everyone.

> Then Jesus answered and said to them, "Most assuredly, I say to you, the Son can do nothing of Himself, but what He sees the Father do; for whatever He does, the Son also

does in like manner. For the Father loves the Son, and shows Him all things that He Himself does; and He will show Him greater works than these, that you may marvel. (John 5:19-20)

Jesus is the only begotten Son of God. He was showing a pattern for other sons and daughters to follow. That is what we should be doing in our lives. We shouldn't be running around trying to make things happen. That is not how life works in God's kingdom.

David had a revelation of the Jerusalem in heaven, and then he manifested it on the earth just as he saw it. He did the same with Mount Zion (2 Samuel 5:6). We all existed in heaven before we arrived on earth. We were called, sanctified, and ordained by God before the foundation of the world.

Every city and nation that God established on the earth has an original blueprint in heaven. Sometimes the current names of the cities that are on the earth won't reflect the actual name God has for them in heaven.

We read in Genesis that when Jacob slept in a place called Luz, he had a dream and an encounter with God. When he woke up, he realized that it was a special place and renamed the place Bethel. He had a revelation of that place as it was in heaven.

> But you have come to Mount Zion and to the city of the living God, the heavenly Jerusalem, to an innumerable company of angels, to the general assembly and church of the firstborn *who are* registered in heaven, to God the Judge of all, to the spirits of just men made perfect, to Jesus the Mediator of the new covenant, and to the blood of sprinkling that speaks better things than *that of* Abel. (Hebrews 12:22-24)

GOD'S PURPOSE AND PATTERN

> For this Hagar is Mount Sinai in Arabia, and corresponds to Jerusalem which now is, and is in bondage with her children—but the Jerusalem above is free, which is the mother of us all. (Galatians 4:24-25)

There are people who were wrongly named, and God had to correct and give them a new name. Likewise, there are places, cities, nations, and people on earth today that were wrongly named and need to be renamed by those who can receive a revelation of their destiny based on who they are in heaven.

God has chosen us in Him to be holy and blameless before the foundation of the world (Ephesians 1:4). The things we see on earth are duplicates and their original is in heaven. Many of the technologies we use today are substitutes of the capabilities we used to have before the fall. For example, airplanes, television, and telephones are a substitute for the spiritual abilities that allowed us to communicate with each other before the fall.

I believe that before the fall we were able to travel to any place on earth or in heaven, at any time, and without the restrictin of time or space. We were not supposed to be limited to time and space. Now the world of technology is trying to come up with a solution for this, but that's not their job. They can only come up with duplicates or substitutes. We could communicate with other people through spirit-to-spirit communication just like we do through a phone device.

Mankind is able to recognize what was available to us before the fall in our spirit, but we are not fully restored yet. We are in the process of restoration. That is why the Bible says to think about things that are in heaven so we can manifest them on the earth (Colossians 3:1-2). It doesn't tell us to go and live there. We were not created to live in heaven. If God wanted all of us there, He would have kept us there.

There is an Eden in heaven. There is a nation of Israel in heaven. That is what He wanted to birth through Abraham. God wanted to transform the entire earth through Abraham and his descendants. That is why when God called Abraham, He told him to leave his place and go to a land that He would show him. That word translated "land" is the same word used for "earth" in Genesis 1:1. In one place it is translated as "earth," and in Genesis 12:3, it is translated as "land."

God wanted to show Abraham the earth through His kingdom perspective—the earth exists in heaven and how this earth is supposed to be. The fall affected the earth, but it did not affect the original earth that is in heaven. So God calls certain people in every generation and gives them a vision of how certain aspects of the earth are supposed to look. Their job is to manifest it on earth as it is in heaven.

Through Christ, God reconciled things in heaven and things on earth so they can become one again in essence and in quality. He reconciled heaven and earth (Ephesians 1:10; Colossians 1:20). Now everything that is in heaven in relation to the earth can manifest on the earth once again. That's how we make this earth a new earth.

Many believers' excuse is if the earth and the world are going to be destroyed, then why should they do anything good on the earth or with their lives other than saving some souls and taking them to heaven? This mindset came about because of the wrong information we received about this world and the earth.

The End of the World or the End of the Age?

The majority of us, who grew up reading the old King James Version of the Bible, have inherited many wrong interpretations and misunderstandings of the Holy Scriptures. One of them is that we have been waiting for the end of this world. But, if we study the Scriptures, we will notice that the Bible does not talk about the end of this world. In every place it is mentioned, the phrase "end of the world" in the King James Version, is a mistranslation of the original word used in the Greek text.

The first place we read the phrase "end of the world" is in Matthew 13:39, "The enemy that sowed them is the devil; the harvest is the **end of the world**; and the reapers are the angels."

The Difference Between the "World" and the "Age"

If we read the above verse in the New King James Version, the word "world" has been replaced by the word "age." The word for world in the Greek is *Kosmos,* and the word for age is *Aeon.* They are entirely two different words with different meanings. ***Kosmos means the system by which this earth and the universe operates. Age or era means a period of time in which God interacts or deals with humans, and the earth, based on a certain method or system.*** Kosmos has to do with the system of operation; age is talking about a particular period of time.

Below are more examples where the phrase "end of the age" is translated incorrectly as "end of the world." Since many believers grew up reading the King James Version of the Bible, because of what they read, they have been waiting for the end of the world. But the ruling family who translated the Bible is not waiting for the end of the world. They will never mention such things. They have set in place successors for their kingdom for the next thousand years, while deceived believers are running around like chickens with their head cut off.

Below are more verses that were mistakenly translated:

> And as he sat upon the mount of Olives, the disciples came unto him privately, saying, Tell us, when shall these things

> be? and what shall be the sign of thy coming, and of the **end of the world**? (Matthew 24:3, KJV)

> Now all these things happened unto them for examples: and they are written for our admonition, upon whom the **ends of the world** are come. (1 Corinthians 10:11, KJV)

> For then must he often have suffered since the foundation of the world: but now once in the **end of the world** hath he appeared to put away sin by the sacrifice of himself. (Hebrews 9:26, KJV)

The Bible talks about the start and the end of different ages or time periods. Theologians call them dispensations. Since the creation of mankind, and the fall, God has dealt with us, and the earth, based on different dispensations or methods. Right now, we are in the dispensation or the age of the kingdom, where God deals with mankind based on His grace.

> The law and the prophets *were* until John. Since that time the kingdom of God has been preached, and everyone is pressing into it. (Luke 16:16)

God's Purposes vs. God's Methods

To correctly interpret the Bible, we need to understand the difference between God's purposes and His methods. God's purposes are eternal, and they never change; His methods, through which He deals with mankind, change from age to age. After Jesus's death and resurrection, the Old Covenant era (age) came to an end, but the world did not come to an end (Luke 16:16). The world is still here, and it will be here tomorrow.

GOD'S PURPOSE AND PATTERN

Our focus should be on the purposes of God, not on the methods. Unfortunately, we neglected His purpose, and instead, we emphasized and focused on the methods. The result we gained from it almost destroyed us. For example, law and grace are methods through which God has interacted with humans. But His purpose, which is to establish His kingdom and will on earth as it is in heaven, remains the same in all ages.

People went after the law and made it their god. The religious leaders began to use the law for their advantage and to oppress people. These days, people run after the teaching of grace the same way, and many worship grace instead of worshipping Jesus.

The disciples asked Jesus a very important question in Matthew 24:3, "And as he sat upon the mount of Olives, the disciples came unto him privately, saying, Tell us, when shall these things be? and what shall be the sign of thy coming, and of the end of the world?" (KJV). Ever since this verse was spoken, we have been waiting for the end of this world. But again, the word "world" is a wrong translation; it is supposed to be "end of the age."

In AD 70, when the temple in Jerusalem was destroyed as Jesus predicted in Matthew 24, that age came to an end, but the world continued to exist. It was the end of *their* world, not the *whole* world. Another verse that talks about the end of the world is Matthew 28:20, "Teaching them to observe all things whatsoever I have commanded you: and, lo, I am with you always, even unto the end of the world. Amen." (KJV)

Again, it should have been translated "end of the age" and not "end of the world." The question is, why did the translators use the wrong word? I believe they did it on purpose to confuse and deceive the common people. It was the practice of the ruling class, and the religious leaders, to use God's Word to take advantage of the people by keeping them ignorant and by misleading them. For centuries, they did not allow common people to even read God's Word.

Now there are plenty of free resources available online for anyone to check, and study, to see if what they are reading in the Bible is the correct translation or not. It is always good to compare more than one translation. We have been waiting for almost two thousand years now for this world to come to an end. The world is still here, and we can wait for another two thousand years and miss out on our purpose.

It is time to focus on the purposes of God! When we partner with Him to fulfill His purposes, He takes personal interest in meeting our needs and protecting us from the evil one. That is why Jesus told us to seek His kingdom and His righteousness first, and then all the things we need will be added to us. May the Lord help us do that.

> Then the seventh angel sounded: And there were loud voices in heaven, saying, "The kingdoms of this world have become *the kingdoms* of our Lord and of His Christ, and He shall reign forever and ever!" (Revelation 11:15)

To understand more about the seven dimensions of our purpose and the civilization that existed on this earth prior to Adam, please read my books: *Purpose, Calling, and Gifts* and *The Gospel of the Kingdom*. To understand the seven eternal purposes of God, please read *God's Original Design*.

Chapter 3

God's Heart for the Nations

> Who shall not fear You, O Lord, and glorify Your name? For You alone are holy. For all nations shall come and worship before You, For Your judgments have been manifested.
> (Revelation 15:4)

God wants nations to manifest what is in heaven on the earth. Each nation has a specific and unique destiny from God. I do not believe there is any nation on the earth today that is fully functioning in its kingdom destiny. There are people in every nation that are fulfilling their kingdom destiny, but God wants their entire nation to function as a kingdom nation.

This will happen only when believers in a country receive the message of the kingdom of God, and they, in turn, are released to fulfill their destiny, eventually releasing the destiny of that nation. That is the vision the Lord gave us as a ministry, and it is the purpose for discipling nations.

The majority of believers are not free to fulfill their kingdom destiny or assignment now. They are stuck serving the devil and his kingdom for money to survive. Many are not even aware that they have a destiny. They were never trained or informed about it.

Each human being was created to fulfill a specific assignment in God's kingdom, however, when they were born in different nations to different families, those nations and families had already been taken captive by the enemy through religion or the Babylonian system.

We are born into slavery by our natural birth—slaves to sin and to the systems of this world. That is why God gave us another chance to be born again into His kingdom. The born-again experience is supposed to set us free to fulfill our kingdom destiny. But that is not the case with most of us because we did not hear the true gospel of the kingdom. That is why Jesus said, "If the Son makes you free, you shall be free indeed" (John 8:36). This is the purpose of being born again through Jesus Christ.

God's Heart and Plan for the Nations

From the beginning of our existence, God wanted nations to serve Him. We read about nations from Genesis to Revelation. God wants all nations serving Him, but how is that possible? Is it even possible in our day and time?

> Ask of Me, and I will give *You* The **nations** *for* Your inheritance, And the ends of the earth *for* Your possession. (Psalm 2:8)

> All the ends of the world Shall remember and turn to the LORD, and all the families of the **nations** shall worship before You. (Psalm 22:27)

> For the kingdom *is* the Lord's, and He rules over the **nations**. (Psalm 22:28)

> Yes, all kings shall fall down before Him; all **nations** shall serve Him. (Psalm 72:11).

> Arise, O God, judge the earth; for You shall inherit all **nations**. (Psalm 82:8)

> All **nations** whom You have made Shall come and worship before You, O Lord, and shall glorify Your name. (Psalm 86:9)

If God wanted all nations to serve Him, is there a single nation that is serving the Lord God today? I can't think of even a little island that is doing so. We have a huge task ahead of us.

The book of Revelation talks about the restoration of nations back to God. It also talks about the process of how it will be achieved. In fact, the word "nation" is mentioned eighteen times in the book of Revelation.

> But hold fast what you have till I come. And he who overcomes, and keeps My works until the end, to him I will give power over the nations. (Revelation 2:25-26)

The reason for all the judgments of God mentioned in the book of Revelation is to bring nations back to Him.

> Who shall not fear You, O Lord, and glorify Your name? For *You* alone *are* holy. For all **nations** shall come and worship before You, For Your judgments have been manifested." (Revelation 15:4)

> And the **nations** of those who are saved shall walk in its light, and the kings of the earth bring their glory and honor into it. (Revelation 21:24)

> In the middle of its street, and on either side of the river, *was* the tree of life, which bore twelve fruits, each *tree* yielding its

fruit every month. The leaves of the tree *were* for the healing of the **nations**. (Revelation 22:2)

How will these nations come to Jesus or become healed? We thought the book of Revelation was about the end of the world and this earth, but it is about nations being saved and healed. In the above verses, we see that God's heart is for all the nations to serve Him.

In light of these verses and background of God's heart for the nations, Jesus gave us the Great Commission. We have limited the Great Commission to saving souls and taking them to heaven, but that is not what Jesus told us to do. He told us to go and disciple nations. Why does He want us to disciple nations? It is because He wants to manifest His kingdom *in* them and *through* them.

> And Jesus came and spoke to them, saying, "All authority has been given to Me in heaven and on earth. Go therefore and make disciples of all the nations, baptizing them in the name of the Father and of the Son and of the Holy Spirit, teaching them to observe all things that I have commanded you; and lo, I am with you always, *even* to the end of the age." Amen. (Matthew 28:18-20)

All authority has been given to Jesus. Authority means the right to rule. Just like God gave the first Adam dominion over all the earth, the Last Adam, Jesus, received the right to rule the earth. But He can't rule now because there is not even one nation that wants to serve Him. As we disciple nations and bring them to the kingdom of God, Jesus will begin to reign over them through His people.

How do we disciple nations? Jesus told us how to do it in Mark 16:

> And He said to them, "Go into all the world and preach the gospel to every creature." (Mark 16:15)

GOD'S HEART FOR THE NATIONS

We disciple nations by going into the world. Jesus did not tell us to stay away from the world but to go into the world.

But you shall receive power when the Holy Spirit has come upon you; and you shall be witnesses to Me in Jerusalem, and in all Judea and Samaria, and to the end of the earth." (Acts 1:8)

In the above verses, Jesus gave us the process of discipling nations, starting with the cities, then the world, and then the nations. Then the whole earth will come under the rule and reign of God.

The diagram on the next page shows the difference between the earth and the world. Earth is the physical planet, and the kosmos is the system by which the earth operates.

Jesus told us to go into the world of politics, media, business, agriculture, and into every component by which a nation and our world is made. There needs to be an extensive training program to train believers to go into the world. That is why we are starting Kingdom Schools in every nation. If you are interested in starting a Kingdom School in your church or town, please contact us. Thank you.

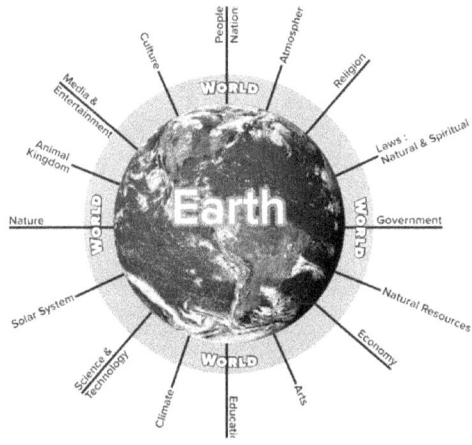

Chapter 4

God's Prototypes

> You are the light of the world. A city that is set on a hill cannot be hidden. (Matthew 5:14)

Why Does God Want a Nation?

A kingdom is a nation, country, or a territory ruled by a king. In our case, our God is King, and He has a kingdom. A kingdom is made of everything a nation is made of. God wants to manifest His kingdom on the earth. It cannot be made visible through one person or a small village, or even a local church. That is why God wants a nation—so that everything that is in His unlimited kingdom can be made manifest, at least on a smaller scale, through this model nation.

Everyone who sees this nation should know what God's kingdom is like and how it operates. That is why He called us the "light of this world," and the nation of Israel "a light to the gentiles." As I said before, light means "blueprint." This means that everyone who wants to know how life and a nation ought to look, should be able to look at us, and the nation of Israel in the Old Testament, and copy us. Imagine what would happen if the whole world were to follow and become like the church in its current state. It would not be good.

Unfortunately, the church and the nation of Israel are not functioning as God designed them to be lights to the gentiles or the world. That is why God wants to re-establish a nation—because His purpose, pattern, principles, and plans remain the same in all ages. Only His methods or processes change from age to age.

To show us what is in His heart for the earth, He decided to establish on the earth exactly what is in heaven. And to show us what He meant by "on earth as it is in heaven," He came down to the earth to establish His kingdom here. The reason He did that is because there were no humans on the earth at that time. He had to prepare everything His son Adam would need before He created him.

The way God works is that for whatever He wants to accomplish, He first establishes a prototype. Then He entrusts it to an individual, his or her family, and the generations to come, to expand and continue the mission God has entrusted to them. Many times, people get stuck, or they stop moving with God. They become traditional, comfortable, or stagnant, and they stop moving with Him. So whatever God started through them, instead of expanding and going to the next level, begins to die out over time.

To show us what it will look like when His kingdom is established on the earth, God gave us three prototypes in the Bible. We are going to briefly examine each one to find out the nature and function of a kingdom nation.

The Garden of Eden - The First Kingdom Nation

What was the *system* God implemented on the earth for mankind to live and to provide for them? Many of God's people today want to leave

GOD'S PROTOTYPES

Babylon to serve God and fulfill their kingdom assignment, but they do not know where to go or how to find the resources to provide for themselves and their families. We are going to see what God's original plan was to provide for Adam and Eve, the first family He started. We were created to live in and expand God's kingdom.

God's purposes are eternal. He created the earth to establish His kingdom, and He entrusted that task to us. From the beginning, God wanted to show mankind how this kingdom of His should look in the natural when it manifests on the earth. He came down and established a garden and put the man in it to tend and to keep it. The garden of Eden was the first prototype of a kingdom nation.

Why did God come down to plant the garden? He could have entrusted the task to an angel or to any number of angels, but when it comes to His kingdom, He takes the initiative and has a personal interest. He wants to make sure it is done exactly the way He wants it. God brought a "piece of heaven" (His kingdom) and planted it on the earth. The Bible calls it the garden of Eden.

Originally, God wanted the entire earth to be like the garden of Eden. That is why God created the earth and humans.

He established the garden as it is in heaven. That is also why God Himself came down to earth to plant the garden.

The garden of Eden was the physical manifestation of the invisible kingdom of God. There was no difference between the garden and heaven. They were the same in both essence and nature. Life in the garden and life in heaven were of the same quality; the garden of Eden was the first Kingdom Nation God established on the earth.

The garden of Eden reflected heaven; it was an extension of heaven. Everything in Eden was done exactly as it was in heaven, so there was no difference between life in heaven and the life manifested in Eden. There is no death in heaven, and Adam was not created to die. As long as mankind lived in Eden, physical death had no power over them. There was no sickness or disease in the garden either. God's will was done in Eden as it was in heaven.

God Himself came and "established" this nation. The Bible says that God came down and planted the garden. "The Lord God planted a garden eastward in Eden" (Genesis 2:8). The word "planted" is not an agricultural word in the original Hebrew language. The word in the Hebrew language for "planted" also means to establish—to build. When you plant a garden, you won't say that you established a garden. But when we say things concerning a city or a nation, we use the word "establish."

There are other places the same word *planted* is used when God started or established a nation.

> You have brought a vine out of Egypt; You have cast out the nations, and planted it. (Psalm 80:8)

Yet I had planted you a noble vine, a seed of highest quality. How then have you turned before Me into the degenerate plant of an alien vine? (Jeremiah 2:21)

Everything a nation is made of was present in the garden of Eden. Below you will see evidence.

Kingdom Agriculture Was There

It is God's responsibility to feed and take care of any type of creation that is doing what He created it to do by remaining in the place He put them. It was God's responsibility to provide for Adam. Not only for Adam, but for the entire human race. That is why Jesus told us to seek His kingdom and righteousness first; then our food, and everything else we need, will be added to us.

Jesus said in Matthew 6:32 that our heavenly Father knows we need all these things to live and do His will. But the majority of believers are not experiencing God's provision because they are not doing what God wants them to do.

> And God said, "See, I have given you every herb *that* yields seed which *is* on the face of all the earth, and every tree whose fruit yields seed; to you it shall be for food. (Genesis 1:29)

> And out of the ground the Lord God made every tree grow that is pleasant to the sight and good for food. (Genesis 2:9)

> And the Lord God commanded the man, saying, "Of every tree of the garden you may freely eat. (Genesis 2:16)

Kingdom Economy Was There

God's kingdom is the wealthiest and richest kingdom in the universe. There is no lack, recession, inflation, or economic crisis in His kingdom. God knew that Adam would need resources to fulfill what He created him to do, so He already deposited everything we need in the earth. We must harness and extract what we need as faithful stewards.

> Now a river went out of Eden to water the garden, and from there it parted and became four riverheads. The name of the first *is* Pishon; it *is* the one which skirts the whole land of Havilah, where *there is* gold. And the gold of that land *is* good. Bdellium and the onyx stone *are* there. (Genesis 2:10-12)

It was God who started a nation's economy based on a gold standard for the first time. It was His idea.

Kingdom Government Was There

What type of government was God envisioning to establish on the earth to govern men? Was it democratic, socialist, capitalist? We will discuss more about this later in the book.

> Then the Lord God took the man and put him in the garden of Eden to tend and keep it. And the Lord God commanded the man, saying, "Of every tree of the garden you may freely eat; but of the tree of the knowledge of good and evil you shall not eat, for in the day that you eat of it you shall surely die." (Genesis 2:15-16)

> Out of the ground the Lord God formed every beast of the field and every bird of the air, and brought *them* to Adam to see what he would call them. And whatever Adam called each living creature, that *was* its name. (Genesis 2:19)

God's idea of government was self-government—each individual connected to Him and led by His Spirit according to their own choice.

Kingdom Education Was There

God did not start a school and then send Adam there to be educated so that someday he could find a job and make a living. Most of the people God used in the Bible were not trained in a school like we know of, but they were all *educated* in different components of the kingdom based on their calling. God trained them in His *kingdom school* through circumstances in their life.

> Then the Lord God took the man and put him in the garden of Eden to tend and keep it. And the Lord God commanded the man, saying, "Of every tree of the garden you may freely eat; but of the tree of the knowledge of good and evil you shall not eat, for in the day that you eat of it you shall surely die." (Genesis 2:15-17)

Anything Adam needed to know, he could learn from God who is the Source of all wisdom, knowledge, and understanding. Adam had to learn how to care for the garden and protect it from the enemy. When the test came, he failed miserably and lost what God had given him.

Kingdom Family Was There

The blueprint for family life was revealed in Genesis. If we do not follow that blueprint, marriage won't work.

> And the Lord God said, "*It is* not good that man should be alone; I will make him a helper comparable to him." (Genesis 2:18)

> And the Lord God caused a deep sleep to fall on Adam, and he slept; and He took one of his ribs, and closed up the flesh in its place. Then the rib which the Lord God had taken from man He made into a woman, and He brought her to the man. And Adam said: "This is now bone of my bones and flesh of my flesh; she shall be call woman, because she was taken out of man." Therefore a man shall leave his father and mother and be joined to his wife, and they shall become one flesh. And they were both naked, the man and his wife, and were not ashamed. (Genesis 2:21-25)

Kingdom Healthcare Was There

Sickness and disease came because of the fall. God included every kind of food humans need to live healthy, and He also intended for food to be our *medicine*. Unfortunately, today, medicine has become people's food. We have to go back to kingdom agriculture to reverse those illnesses that are prevalent among us today. They won't be cured by medicine, but they can be cured by a change of diet.

> And out of the ground the Lord God made every tree grow that is pleasant to the sight and good for food. (Genesis 2:9)

God included the remedy for every sickness or disease we might face in the plant kingdom. The tilling of the land did not start until after the curse. Man did not need to till the ground to plant; the earth had a built-in system to sustain itself and produce what we need.

Adam failed in his mission and lost the garden, the first kingdom nation God established. With the garden, we lost the blueprint. God's purpose remains the same, so He decided to reintroduce it by creating the second prototype of a king- dom nation.

The Nation of Israel - The Second Kingdom Nation

After Adam failed and humans multiplied, from time to time, God would call an individual to a mountain or to a place in the Spirit to show them what is in heaven. Then it was that person's responsibility to go and manifest what he saw. That is why God wants everyone that is born again to see His kingdom (John 3:3).

When God called Abraham, the first promise He gave to him was that He would make him a great nation. Why a great nation? Why did God want a nation again? The reason is as we saw before: He wanted to manifest His kingdom on the earth, and to manifest His kingdom, He needs a nation—a prototype for other nations and people to follow.

God did not say to Abraham that He would make him a great city, church, choir, or make him rich; He promised him a nation. The thing that fascinated me most was that the first requirement for Abraham to become this great nation was to go to the land that God was going to show him.

God wanted the entire earth to be like heaven. He wanted the whole earth to be filled with His glory. And He wanted all the nations to come and worship before Him (Psalm 86:9). He had to begin somewhere, so He called Abraham and entrusted him with this vision.

That is why God promised that he would be a blessing to all the families of the earth—not just one nation, but every single family of the earth. Nations are made of families. Again, God wanted to establish another prototype nation for other nations to see and copy to experience the same blessings and favor from God. All they need to do is agree to become a kingdom nation for God to manifest His kingdom and glory on the earth.

A Heavenly Pattern

The word "nation" in Latin also means to give birth or to be born. God wanted Abraham to conceive something in the spirit and then give birth to it. He wanted him to conceive the earth from a heavenly perspective and give birth to a kingdom nation.

God told Abraham to get out of his country, family, and his father's house and go to a land He was going to show him. That word "land" in Hebrew is the same word that is used for the earth in Genesis 1:1. We could read it as *in the beginning, God created earth or land.*

THE BIRTHING OF A KINGDOM NATION

God showed Abraham in the spirit how the earth should look from a kingdom perspective—how God wanted the earth to be from the beginning. Abraham saw how the earth should look when God's kingdom is established on the earth. God imprinted in Abraham's spirit the original blueprint for the earth. To bring that vision to fulfillment, He started with one nation through him. God birthed that kingdom nation through Abraham to create the next prototype.

The same pattern of Eden is used here also. The only difference is that it was God who came down to establish Eden because there was no man on the earth at that time. It was Adam's responsibility to copy what God did in Eden and expand it to make the entire earth look like Eden. Eden was the starting point; the end of the earth is the finishing point.

In Abraham's case, God also started with a nation, but it was not the finishing point. That nation was to be the starting point, or the prototype, until the entire earth becomes like the nation that God established. All other nations could see, learn, and copy what God did for Israel and become like them. They were supposed to be the light to the gentiles.

That is why God promised Abraham that in him all the families of the earth would be blessed. The calling was global— to the end of the earth. The same pattern is applied for the nation of the church. It started in Jerusalem, but it was never supposed to end there. They were supposed to take what they received to the end of the earth. That is what Jesus told them to do in Acts 1:8.

> Indeed He says, 'It is too small a thing that You should be My Servant To raise up the tribes of Jacob, And to restore the preserved ones of Israel; I will also give You as a light to the Gentiles, That You should be My salvation to the ends of the earth.' (Isaiah 49:6)

GOD'S PROTOTYPES

> The Gentiles shall come to your light, And kings to the brightness of your rising. (Isaiah 60:3)

God wanted to make Abraham a blessing to all the families of the earth, not just the Jewish race. It was meant to happen through his seed. Jesus Christ is that seed. Through faith in Jesus, we became the seed of Abraham. Through us, God wants to bless the entire earth. Our calling is always to the earth or to do something on the earth. God never called a human to do anything for Him in heaven.

After hundreds of years, that promise was fulfilled, though Abraham did not live to see the fulfillment of that promise. His great grandchildren became that nation. We know the history of Israel. More than half of the Bible is about them and what happened to them.

They were the most blessed nation on earth. While they were in the wilderness, God was preparing them to function as a nation. He implemented each component of a nation, as it is in heaven. They had their own education system, economy, judicial system, agriculture, moral, and healthcare system.

God specifically told them what kind of nation He wanted Israel to be. We read that in the following verses.

> Now therefore, if you will indeed obey My voice and keep My covenant, then you shall be a special treasure to Me above all people; for all the earth *is* Mine. And you shall be to Me a **kingdom of priests and a holy nation.** (Exodus 19:5-6)

The above verses are very important because they are the blueprint for how the nation of Israel should function. God wanted them to function as a kingdom of priests and a holy nation. In other words, He wanted them to be a royal priesthood and a holy nation. Please keep these verses close to your heart because we will need them again when I explain about the church.

They traded with other nations and kingdoms once they were established as a nation. We should trade with other nations and kingdoms to multiply the wealth God has given us, and also to bring the wealth of the wicked into the kingdom nation. All wealth and resources that God created must be used to build His kingdom. They did not borrow anything from the world, neither Egypt nor Babylon. And they did not send their children to be educated by Babylon.

Israel Rejects God's Design

The nation of Israel was the second prototype for every other nation to duplicate and follow, but they kept it for themselves. They began to play spiritual superiority and abused and enslaved other nations. Not only that; the worst crime they committed was forsaking their God and King, as they went and worshipped other gods.

When Israel rejected God and His kingdom assignment, He took that same blueprint and gave it to another nation. Remember, God's purpose never changes, but His methods change from time to time. I will tell you more about this nation in a minute.

When the nation of Israel failed in their mission, God decided to create another nation. This nation also has the same purpose and pattern as the nation of Israel. The only difference is this nation is made of people from every other nation and tongue on the face of the earth. Anyone can become a citizen of this nation. All they are required to do is to believe in Jesus Christ.

As I explained before, whether it was the garden of Eden, the nation of Israel, or the nation of the church, God has the same purpose for all of them. He launched all three of them to establish His kingdom and will on earth. When people rejected His kingdom agenda, He rejected them also.

GOD'S PROTOTYPES

> But woe to you, scribes and Pharisees, hypocrites! For you shut up the kingdom of heaven against men; for you neither go in *yourselves,* nor do you allow those who are entering to go in. (Matthew 23:13)

> Woe to you lawyers! For you have taken away the key of knowledge. You did not enter in yourselves, and those who were entering in you hindered. (Luke 11:52)

They did not care about the people, nor their God. The same thing happened to the church. We lost our purpose and began to build cathedrals and denominations based on the personal interpretations of the Word by different ministers. Those who had the biggest following and the biggest building were thought to be the most spiritual. They did not understand God's purpose for the earth and mankind because they missed God's purpose. Jesus told the religious leaders this:

> Therefore I say to you, the kingdom of God will be taken from you and given to a nation bearing the fruits of it. (Matthew 21:43)

Jesus told them the kingdom of God will be taken from them, which means their purpose will be taken from them. Why? They were called to establish God's kingdom on earth and to take His salvation to the ends of the earth. They were supposed to be the light to the gentiles, showing them what it means to live for God and how to fulfill His purpose. They failed on all fronts, and God had enough with them.

When your kingdom assignment is taken from you, you need to fill that place with something else to keep people busy. Religion, traditions, and entertainment are some of the things people use now to fill the place of God's kingdom purpose.

Israel became a nation without purpose. They built synagogues all over and traveled land and sea to proselyte the people to become

Jews. They taught them Judaism. Jesus was not happy with any of their accomplishments. Finally, He became tired of their temple, and said it would be torn down from its foundation. That temple had become a den of thieves and a place that collected taxes from worshippers, for the people in power.

If someone did not pay the temple tax, they were not allowed to go into the temple to worship God. They did not allow gentiles to come near the temple. It should have been a house of prayer for all nations. It sounds like many of today's churches and influential ministers.

Which nation is Jesus talking about in the above verse? Let's find that out.

The Church - The Third Kingdom Nation

Why did God come up with an idea called "church?" What was in the mind of Jesus when He said He will build His Ekklesia? Theologians have come up with all sorts of ideas and interpretations on the church and why God launched a venture called church on earth. Religion made us believe that Jesus started the church to save people and take them to heaven after they die. Neither Jesus nor the early apostles preached such a gospel during their earthly ministry.

I have read and heard many theologians say that the church was an unplanned endeavor or an interim plan of God for a certain period of time. It is like couples having an unplanned conception. God and His kingdom do not operate like that. God declares the end from the beginning. He is all-knowing. He already planned out everything in eternity, and nothing can challenge or withstand His plans and purposes. He may use detours and delays, depending on the cooperation of mankind, but His purpose remains the same in eternity and throughout all generations.

Otherwise, we wouldn't be able to trust Him or rely on His promises. If He kept changing them, His Word also would change. But the Bible clearly says that His Word is established in heaven forever. It also says that Jesus Christ, who is the Word made flesh, is the same yesterday, today, and forever. The church was part of God's idea from the beginning because He wants all nations to serve Him, not just the Jews.

Understanding the Ekklesia

The reason we think the church was unplanned is because of its name. We don't see the word "church" used in the Old Testament. That is also a misunderstanding. In the original text, the word "church" is NOT used anywhere in the Bible, in either the New or Old Testament. It was an adopted or made-up word by Bible translators to confuse the people. Neither Jesus nor the apostles ever used the word "church" when they spoke or in their writings.

However, the concept and meaning of the church is present throughout the Bible. From Genesis to the book of Revelation, we can see that it was always in the heart of God. He always wanted a *church* to administer His kingdom on the earth. He never wanted a religion or a religious institution representing Him.

That is why, as a ministry, we don't use the word "church" very much; instead, we use the Greek word *Ekklesia* to bring out its original meaning and intent. The concept of the word Ekklesia, or church, was used in the Old Testament times. When Stephen was preaching about the people of Israel in the wilderness, he used the word Ekklesia in Acts 7:38. I explained the purpose and function of the Ekklesia in detail in a previous chapter.

Ekklesia is an Old Testament Hebrew concept, not a Greek idea, and the word "church" is not an accurate translation. The word "church" is pagan in its origin, but because we grew up hearing the word over and over, it became part of our paradigm and mindset. If we could talk to a first-century believer about the word "church," they wouldn't have any idea what we are talking about because they never heard that word before.

Why Jesus Started the Ekklesia

Now the question is, what is a church or an Ekklesia, and why did Jesus start it? Again, God never changes His purpose. Throughout the history of the earth, He has had only one major purpose, which is to establish His kingdom and will on earth as it is in heaven.

One of the most important truths I have discovered by the help of the Holy Spirit is whether it was Eden, Israel, or the Ekklesia/church God launched, all of them have the same purpose: to establish His kingdom and will on earth; to overthrow the gates of hell and its assignments; and to prevent Satan and his kingdom from having any root in any nation on the earth. That is His agenda and master plan.

God uses different methods and names throughout the ages, depending on the times and seasons we are living in. God never intended for Eden, Israel, or the church to become a "rescue boat" for people to reach heaven. No, instead they were *vehicles* through which God wanted to manifest heaven and His will on earth. They are nations through which He wanted to express His kingdom, His heart, His power, His glory, and the riches of His grace and mercy to the rest of the world—and His wisdom to the principalities and powers in the heavenly places.

If there is no kingdom of God, there is no reason for us to exist. If the church is not manifesting and administering God's kingdom on the earth, there is no reason for such a church to exist. It will disappear over time.

What most do not understand is that God wants His church to function as a nation. We do not have any problem accepting that Israel was and is a nation, but it is difficult for us to comprehend how on earth the church can function as a nation, and is it even biblical? I will show you from Scripture that God wants the church to function as a nation, and that is what He called it.

When we think of church, a certain picture comes to our mind, usually, a building with people inside singing or listening to a preacher. Is that the concept Jesus had in His mind when He said He will build His Ekklesia, or church? How many worship services like the ones we know today did Jesus and His disciples conduct?

The reason we do not understand the kingdom of God is because we grew up hearing more about the church, revival, and rapture than about the kingdom. In the disciples' case, what they heard the majority of the time from Jesus was about the kingdom of God.

If we are to understand the purpose and function of the church, we need to understand the kingdom of God. Jesus spent three years teaching the disciples about the kingdom before He introduced them to the church because He knew that if they did not understand the kingdom of God, they could not understand the purpose of the church, or they would misuse it. When Jesus told them about the church, they were ready for it, at least from a natural perspective.

God called the people of Israel out of Egypt to become a kingdom of priests and a holy nation. They were the Ekklesia in the Old Testament. We are a called-out and chosen generation, just like they were. God wanted them to become a nation because that is what He promised their forefather Abraham.

Lost Purpose

When explaining the church, the New Testament uses the same phrases and blueprint that are used for the nation of Israel. They were called a nation made of kings and priests. We are also called a nation that is made of kings and priests. We have the same purpose and the same function, so we wonder how the church ended up the way it is today.

The same thing that happened to the nation of Israel happened to us. They lost their purpose, and we lost ours. They began to build synagogues all across the nation to promote personal interpretations and teachings of the law of Moses by different Rabbis. They began to compete for influence, power, and control over people. Their motive was to show who had the latest and the most lucrative interpretation of God's Word in order to rob the people.

> Therefore I say to you, the kingdom of God will be taken from you and given to a nation bearing the fruits of it. (Matthew 21:43)

> Which nation is Jesus referring to in the above verse? To which nation did He give the kingdom of God? He reveals that in Luke 12:32:

> Do not fear, little flock, for it is your Father's good pleasure to give you the kingdom.

Jesus was speaking to His disciples. The Father is pleased to give us the kingdom. I hope we won't miss His purpose this time. God has been waiting for the church now for over two thousand years. We have done everything else except what God wants us to do. In another place, He said:

> Just as my Father has given me a kingdom, I also give you a kingdom. (Luke 22:29, NCV)

GOD'S PROTOTYPES

> Another translation says, "As My Father has given Me a holy nation, I will give you the right." (NLV)

> The Gentiles shall see your righteousness, And all kings your glory. You shall be called by a new name, which the mouth of the Lord will name. (Isaiah 62:2)

The above verses are talking about the new nation Jesus came to start—the Ekklesia. He followed the same pattern to start this nation as the Old Testament nation of Israel was started. But He called us with a new name. Israel was started with twelve men, and this new kingdom nation He also started with twelve men.

> But you *are* a chosen generation, a royal priesthood, a holy nation, His own special people, that you may proclaim the praises of Him who called you out of darkness into His marvelous light. (1 Peter 2:9)

Peter uses the same phrases for the church that God used to describe the nation of Israel in Exodus 19:5-6. They were a chosen people out of the whole earth. We, the church, are a chosen generation. They were called out from Egypt. We are the called-out ones. They were a kingdom of priests. We, the church, are a kingdom or a royal priesthood. They were a holy nation, and we, the church, are a holy nation.

How did the people of Israel function as a kingdom of priests and a holy nation? That is exactly the way the church is supposed to function today. There shouldn't be any difference whatsoever. So what happened to the church? We became fragmented into millions of pieces because we lost the kingdom of God, which is our purpose—just like the nation of Israel lost it.

Israel became a nationalistic, political, and religious movement without the kingdom purpose. They began to fight and promote their religiosity across the globe. Even today, there are plenty of Judaizers who are trying to convert gullible Christians to follow the law of Moses or some traditions of men. We should run from such deception. Any teaching, or anyone that doesn't promote the kingdom of God, is promoting deception from the enemy. It is nothing but religion.

The Parallel Between Eden, Israel, and the Church

Our God is a God of purpose, patterns, principles, and plans.

Purpose means original intent. Before we start living our life, it is important to understand why God created the earth and then put us here. Until and unless we understand that, our life will not make any sense. At the end, we will say that everything is meaningless. That is what happened to Solomon, the wisest man that ever lived on the earth.

We did not understand the parallel between Eden, Israel, and the church. That is where we went terribly wrong in our understanding and interpretation of the Bible. We must understand the relationship between the three.

We treated them independently and separately, as if one has no connection with the other. That is why we have created so many divisions among humanity based on different belief systems, based on color and race, and in the church, based on how an individual interpreted a certain verse.

The Bible is not given to us for private interpretation. We must look at God's Word based on the big picture and purpose.

> Knowing this first, that no prophecy of Scripture is of any private interpretation. (2 Peter 1:20)

GOD'S PROTOTYPES

We have fabricated so many fables and misinterpretations of God's Word and created confusion. Now the majority of the people in the church do not know their purpose. Can you imagine that? God's own people, who believe and worship the Creator, do not understand why He created them. What is more pathetic than that?

God didn't create Eden or Israel to take people to heaven. Neither did He start the church to do that. This might shock every religious bone that is in you. All three were personally initiated and directed by God in their establishment. As we saw before, Eden was planted or established by God.

Once He establishes something, He implements systems, laws, and precepts. These are the principles by which His creation is sustained so that what He started remains and functions as He intended.

Eden, Israel, and the church are different systems, vehicles, or prototypes that God has established to accomplish His purpose on earth. He calls them nations. He uses different names just like nations have different names. If these entities are not fulfilling God's purpose, they are wasting their time, resources, and energy. God is looking at the fruit we produce, not at the leaves and branches.

Here is where the church went wrong: we thought that if we plant more churches in a city or a nation, things will change for the better. That is not true. Jesus did not commission His apostles to go out and plant churches everywhere. We have created so many para church organizations and denominations focused on church planting that waste a lot of resources and destinies and don't fulfill God's purpose.

Organizations and denominations thrive on telling others how many churches and workers they have under their banner—if they only knew why Jesus started His Ekklesia. There is no way to measure the amount of money and resources that have gone wasted throughout the years.

THE BIRTHING OF A KINGDOM NATION

What will bring unity among God's people? Not another revival, but coming to an understanding about our purpose.

Purpose unites people. When we have a common vision, then we can join our hearts and hands to accomplish it.

We shouldn't get stuck on minor things or how a person interprets a certain verse. When we look at life from heaven and with a kingdom perspective, everything will make sense. It doesn't matter which water you get baptized in or what time of the day you take communion, or the type of building you gather in. The truth is that he who has the Son has eternal life.

> He who believes in Him is not condemned; but he who does not believe is condemned already, because he has not believed in the name of the only begotten Son of God. (John 3:18)

> He who believes in the Son has everlasting life; and he who does not believe the Son shall not see life, but the wrath of God abides on him. (John 3:36)

According to the above verses, whoever believes in Jesus, regardless of their outward appearance, will end up in heaven.

God does not save or condemn people based on their appearance but based on their belief.

As I mentioned in my other books, Genesis chapters 1 and 2 are God's original blueprint for life on earth. His purpose, pattern, principles, and plans are clearly revealed in those chapters. Everything God does, either through Israel or the church, is to bring humans and the earth back to that original plan.

Operation of the Kingdom Nation

A kingdom nation starts within a nation, as a mustard seed, and then infiltrates and influences the systems around it, slowly but surely, like leaven or yeast does, until the whole lump is leavened. Seeds and yeast remain invisible until the right time comes. A kingdom nation will continue to grow and expand both covertly and overtly until that whole natural nation comes under the influence of God and His kingdom.

Religion and religious spirits make so much noise when they go into a region. They exaggerate numbers and manipulate people's emotions for their personal gain. The kingdom of God does not operate like that. The kingdom of God is an invisible or spiritual kingdom, and it does not make any noise until it manifests in the natural. By the time it manifests, it will be too late for anyone to prevent it from happening. You cannot stop a seed from growing when it falls into the right environment. Growth is a natural by-product.

I only visited Israel once. I saw the Jordan river and the spot where most people take baptism. It is one of the dirtiest bodies of water I have ever seen in my life. People believe that if they can be dipped in that water, something special will happen to them, or God will love or accept them more. These are all belief systems that stem from the religious spirit and have nothing to do with God or His kingdom.

If God is to manifest His kingdom through the church, then, as we saw, the church must function as a nation. Below are some parallels between the nation of Israel and the nation of the Church:

- Both are called nations
- Both are called Israel (Galatians 6:6)
- Both are made of kings and priests

THE BIRTHING OF A KINGDOM NATION

- Both are supposed to be a light to the gentiles, or the world
- Both have the same purpose
- Both were established by God through twelve men
- God wanted to be the King of both

Chapter 5

The Process of Becoming a Kingdom Nation—Part 1

I will make you a great nation; I will bless you and make your name great; and you shall be a blessing. (Genesis 12:2)

God always calls His people out of something before they can become a part of His mission on the earth. Then He makes them a nation, or whatever He wants them to be. First, we need to come out of where we currently are, in order to become something new. It's not easy, and many are not willing to do that.

We are all born into this world system that is controlled by various elements such as religion, culture, politics, mammon (money), etc. God cannot use us while we still have the mindset that was formed in us by these elements, so He calls us to come out of them to be a part of His kingdom nation.

To God, the change that needs to happen in the way we think is more important than any physical relocation. The purpose of relocation is to cause a shift in the way we think.

THE BIRTHING OF A KINGDOM NATION

Now the Lord had said to Abram: "Get out of your country, From your family and from your father's house, to a land that I will show you." (Genesis 12:1)

Therefore

"Come out from among them and be separate, says the Lord. Do not touch what is unclean, and I will receive you. I will be a Father to you, and you shall be My sons and daughters, says the LORD Almighty." (2 Corinthians 6:17-18)

And I heard another voice from heaven saying, "Come out of her, my people, lest you share in her sins, and lest you receive of her plagues." (Revelation 18:4)

Both Old and New Testaments require that we come out or leave something to become a part of God's agenda.

There are mainly two systems or nations that we are required to come out of to step into God's kingdom nation.

In the above verses, God is calling His people to come out of Babylon. Once we come out, we are a *called-out* people—an Ekklesia. We were not created to build Babylon with our sweat and blood. We were created to build God's kingdom and serve Him all the days of our lives.

Egypt and Babylon

There are two nations mentioned from Genesis to Revelation that are very significant to understand. They are not just two historic nations, but demonic systems the devil uses to enslave God's people, in every generation, so they won't discover God's kingdom or fulfill their purpose.

THE PROCESS OF BECOMING A KINGDOM NATION—PART 1

These two nations are Egypt and Babylon. There is a specific reason they are mentioned from Genesis to Revelation. Egypt represents a religious system. It was the birthplace of various religions, magic, sorcery, witchcraft, and mind control. The purpose of religion is mind control—to enslave humans so they become addicted to rituals and superstitions contrary to the kingdom of God.

Conversely, Babylon is a political and economic system. It includes all sorts of fun, human achievements, and political systems. It is built on humanism, and it offers a false sense of freedom and ownership. People think they can do whatever they want to do when they want to do it. That is not true freedom. True freedom is when you are free to do what you were born to do.

Jesus was a free man, but He was not running around doing His own thing whenever He wanted. He came to do the will of His Father. So Egypt represents the religious spirit, and Babylon represents the spirit of this world. One enslaves God's people and the other takes them captive. They are two branches, or wings, of the kingdom of darkness. If the devil cannot enslave an individual with the religious system, he will use the Babylonian system to deceive them. Many people have been taken captive by the glitters and fun of Babylon.

Babylon is the birthplace of all types of humanistic thinking and achievements. It is self-worship; people become their own god. They will not acknowledge God or any authority above them. In Egypt, people worshipped different gods, demons, and idols. In Babylon, man becomes the center of everything and is worshipped as a god. It is the birthplace of all sports, entertainment, and technologies that distract people from God and His purpose.

If we look at the world today, these spirits are prevalent from east to west. When we study the system of rulership of these two kingdoms, we have more understanding about how they operated. In Egypt, the rulers were called pharaohs; it was a title, like pope in the Catholic church. In Babylon, the rulers did not have a particular title; they had individual names.

The intent of both systems is to enslave God's people and keep them as captives, making them dependent on it, instead of God's kingdom, and blinding them from seeing it and knowing their purpose.

Egypt and Babylon were physical nations, but they also represent two demonic systems or entities that have been operating since Genesis. We read about them in Revelation as well. In the book of Revelation, Jerusalem, the city where Jesus died, is called Egypt because it is under the bondage of religion (Revelation 11:8).

The majority of believers are stuck in religion and in Babylon, and they are not free to build God's kingdom. Now when believers hear the gospel of the kingdom and understand about their assignment, they don't know what to do. Many want to leave what they are doing but are concerned about how they will provide for themselves and their families.

If they leave their profession, or their current job, they might become homeless and end up on the street because they don't know where to go or what to do. The reason is because the kingdom nation is not established. Once the kingdom nation is established, every child of God will have a place to serve Him and become part of His dream team.

In order to form this kingdom nation, God's people are required to come out of Egypt and Babylon. As we have seen, they both represent two systems. Again, the majority are stuck and have been taken captive by these forces. We cannot keep one foot in the kingdom of God and the other in one of these systems. Either we serve God and build His kingdom, or we serve the devil and build his kingdom.

THE PROCESS OF BECOMING A KINGDOM NATION—PART 1

How does a kingdom nation look and function in this day and age? Actually, it will be just like how the nation of Israel existed and operated. From the king to the peasant in the field, everyone was serving God and fulfilling their God-given assignment. The king was called and appointed by God, and so was the farmer in the field. Everyone was a part of God's nation and was serving Him from small to great.

As a nation, they were completely dominating the land and bringing the best out of it. They were a light to the gentiles, and they did not give the enemy any foothold. Every time someone committed a crime or a sin, there was a judicial system in place to deal with and purge it.

In Revelation 18:2, we read about the fall of Babylon the great. Before God can judge Babylon, the kingdom nation must come into existence. Otherwise, when Babylon falls, God's people will fall with it because they are dependent on it for everything.

This kingdom nation that God is forming now is without borders and limits. It is a global nation that exists within every nation. The more people understand and fulfill their calling, the more the kingdom of God will begin to infiltrate and influence, and eventually take over the whole nation, as Jesus said in His parables about how the kingdom of heaven operates. It operates like a mustard seed and leaven first.

The kingdom nation is a place where believers from every nation come together to form this new nation under their King, Jesus Christ, and join together with other fellow members of the body, like the Bible says in Ephesians 4:16, "From whom the whole body, joined and knit together by what every joint supplies, according to the effective working by which every part does its share, causes growth of the body for the edifying of itself in love."

This is also a prophetic picture of what we read in the book of Ezekiel—the dry bones coming to life, joining together and becoming an exceedingly great army (Ezekiel 37:1-10).

The New Testament names this called-out people an Ekklesia. It also talks about the various functions and responsibilities of an Ekklesia in fulfilling God's purpose on the earth, which is to establish God's kingdom and will on the earth by forming a kingdom nation. Just like the word "dominion" is a complex word, Ekklesia is a complex word with more than one meaning and function. Following are seven of them that I list and explain in this chapter and the next.

1. Kingdom Context

The first time the word Ekklesia is used in the New Testament is in the context of a kingdom and a political confrontation: a king *building* his Ekklesia to withstand and cancel out the operations of another kingdom. It was a confrontation between two kingdoms: His church and the gates of Hades. In this case, the two kingdoms are spiritual kingdoms. Both are fighting to occupy the earth and for the souls of humans. They are the kingdom of God and the kingdom of darkness. Jesus said:

> I will build My church (*ekklesia*), and the gates of Hades shall not prevail against it. (Matthew 16:18)

When Jesus mentioned the church for the first time, the disciples were not surprised. They did not take Him aside and ask Him for further direction, like they did when He taught them how to pray. When we think of the church today, we think of a building with a cross on the top, or we picture a gathering of people singing or listening to a preacher. I wonder what picture came to the minds of the disciples when they first heard the word *church (Ekklesia)* from Jesus.

When Jesus referred to the church for the first time, He mentioned two things: the fact that He would build it and the idea that there was a battle going on in which they had the authority to prevail. In other words, the number one priority of the church is to prevail in the age-old battle that has been raging over the earth between the kingdom of God and the kingdom of darkness.

This battle is for the gates of the earth. What happens on the earth is determined by which kingdom is possessing the gates. A gate is something that gives or denies access, something that permits or forbids access. God wants His people to possess the gates, but now the enemy is occupying those gates.

It is similar to the situation in the promised land that the people of Israel went in to possess. When they arrived, enemies (giants) were occupying the land. They had to dispossess the enemy. That is what the church (Ekklesia) is supposed to be doing on the earth: uprooting the operation of the enemy and occupying the gates. That is our primary goal.

Another reason the disciples did not question Jesus about the church when He mentioned it, was because they were familiar with the concept of kings and kingdoms having an Ekklesia. From a historical perspective, Israel was a kingdom; and from the political climate in which they were living, Ekklesia was a word used by governments.

They knew that Jesus was a King and that every king needs an Ekklesia. That made sense to them. Every king *calls out* certain citizens to help him administer the affairs of his kingdom. They were called an Ekklesia. Ekklesia was a political term used in the Greek world, and it was never used to address a group of people who *worshipped, preached,* or *sang.*

It was used to represent a group of men who were called out from among the people by a king or government to administer the political, judicial, economic, and social affairs and policies of the kingdom, to the people and for the people. They executed the will and plan of the king in the kingdom.

Every king and kingdom had an Ekklesia that governed its affairs. Jesus added a spiritual dimension to His kingdom and Ekklesia when He said, "I will build My church," because His kingdom is a spiritual kingdom. He did not say He would build a worship center, temple, synagogue, or even a cathedral. Jesus is the King, and He has a kingdom, so He needs an Ekklesia to govern the affairs of His kingdom. That is why He started the church.

They are called elders and governors (elders and bishops in the New Testament). Their job is to see that the will of the king is accomplished in the kingdom or in the territories where the kingdom has influence or jurisdiction.

Before we understand more about the church, it is very important to have an idea of the big picture of what God's plan has been all along. God is a King, and He has a kingdom that He wants to establish on the earth through man— that is His ultimate plan and objective.

Everything He does is geared toward accomplishing that one purpose and nothing else. He wants to reveal His wisdom, glory, and power to the people on the earth as well as to the principalities and powers in the heavenly places (Ephesians 3:10).

Mankind has not come into alignment with God's plan yet— especially the church, which was built to administer the kingdom. Jesus wouldn't have started His church if there was no kingdom to administer. If there was no kingdom, there was no need to set up a governing body. If there is a government, there has to be a nation to govern. If there is no nation to govern, there is no need for a government. Imagine a nation without a government.

The kingdom of God and the church became alienated one from the other. The church has been operating without the kingdom, and the kingdom of God does not have a governing body to administer the will of God on the earth. That is why God seems powerless in what is happening on the earth. He is not able to do what He wants to do because the church is taken over by the religious spirit; they have invented their own programs and are waiting to disappear from the earth.

The person whom the king sends out to expand his territory, rule, and influence to a new region is called an apostle. The term "apostle" also was a political term during Jesus's time. Imagine that; "kingdom" is a political term as well, but we made it into a religion. Many apostles these days are busy building their own ministries and churches.

Before a kingdom community can be established in a new territory, certain preparations and precautions need to be applied. The question is, how do we identify and destroy the gates of hell that are operating in a location, region, or even a nation? First, we need to obtain spiritual clearance.

Obtaining Spiritual Security Clearance

If we need to visit a person of influence or a head of state, the more detailed the security clearance we need to go through. Especially when a person wants to run for a presidential or prime ministerial office, the background check they need to go through is very intense and thorough. If they find anything that is derogatory or any disqualifying factors, their enemies can use it against them and defeat them. They need to obtain security clearance.

Why did Jesus make dealing with the gates of hell and destroying their assignments the primary purpose of the Ekklesia? The world and the earth have been taken over by the enemy and his dark kingdom. Adam surrendered his birthright, and the right to rule this planet, to the devil.

THE BIRTHING OF A KINGDOM NATION

Jesus came to take back what the enemy stole from Adam. The penalty or the wages of sin is death. We were all destined to die; but instead of killing everyone, and because sin came into this world through the disobedience of one man, God decided to rectify sin also by the obedience and death of one Man.

Where the first Adam failed, the Last Adam, Jesus Christ, came and reversed everything that was done wrong by the first Adam. That is why Jesus had to die on the cross. Just as when Adam sinned, we sinned with him, when Jesus died on the cross, we died with Him (Romans 6:8; Colossians 2:12-13). Then when He was resurrected, we were raised up with Him. Right now, we are seated in Him in the heavenly places (Ephesians 2:6).

Any works that we do in any country for God's kingdom, the first thing we need to do is get the spiritual clearance from both the kingdom of heaven and from the kingdom of darkness. Where many people go wrong is, just because they have a passion or a dream, or even if they heard from God, they go ahead and start building without obtaining the spiritual clearance.

What happens as a result is what they build does not last. Or they face immense opposition from the enemy, and they quit before they finish what they started. The enemy comes in within a matter of time, through people within or from outside, and topples or destroys that work. This happened to me personally many times. I thought that all I needed was a vision and some resources. Let me tell you something honestly, just normal prayer is not enough when it comes to establishing God's kingdom and will on earth or in a region. Why?

Every inch of this planet earth has been claimed by the enemy and his cohorts for centuries. We do not know the spiritual history of a region, territory, or a nation, or the legal rights the enemy has over that

THE PROCESS OF BECOMING A KINGDOM NATION—PART 1

people and region. Ignorance is the biggest weapon the enemy uses to keep us blind, ineffective, and defeated.

To go to a foreign country, we need to obtain certain documents and clearance. Passports, visas, and police and health clearance are some of these documents. They want to know that we are not going to be a danger to anyone and that we will not get involved in any illegal activity when we arrive there. Not only that, but they also want to know that you are not trying to escape from any illegal activities or legal claims over your life. They want to know that you are legally and physically free and healthy to travel.

Before I came to the United States for the first time, I had to present a police and health clearance, and especially when I applied for permanent residence status. The government of the United States wanted to make sure I had no criminal background or pending legal claims over my life, and that I did not have any transmittable diseases.

The same principle applies in the spirit world. When we go into a new territory to do anything that God has called us to do, we first need to make sure there is nothing in our lives that belongs to the kingdom of darkness: no sin or illegal or deceitful activities that will give the enemy an open door to come in and cause disruption.

Second, we need to identify the things that are giving the enemy and his kingdom legal grounds or rights to operate in that region—who or what has opened the gate for the enemy that gave him legal right to operate. This is how we identify the gates of hell that are operating there.

Whatever gives legal right to any spirit being to operate on the earth is called a gate. Our body, in fact, all physical bodies were created to make spirits legal on the earth. Now there are systems (religion, business, government, education, media, etc.), objects, places, creatures, and people that give the enemy the legal right to execute the will of Satan.

That is why Jesus mentioned dealing with the gates of hell as the primary responsibility of the Ekklesia in a region. Unless we follow this divine protocol, we are asking for trouble. Because God's people don't follow this protocol, they fail in their mission, and then they blame God or become disappointed, or they quit.

The same mistake happened to Adam. He did not secure and fortify the potential gates by subduing and taking dominion over the creatures God mentioned in Genesis 1:26. Those creatures were the potential gates for the enemy because they were the ones with physical bodies.

When Jesus came the first time to this earth, He was only sent to the lost sheep of Israel. The Father did not authorize Him to go to any other country or to deal with any other people groups. That is why He was very hesitant when people from other cultures or nationalities came to Him for help. He had to make sure they received the spiritual clearance before He could heal them or help them.

One of the things that pleases God is faith. When people exercise faith in the God of Israel, He will show compassion and meet their need. The Bible says that without faith it is impossible to please God (Hebrews 11:6). When they demonstrated faith, through what they spoke, Jesus moved with compassion and met their needs.

How do we obtain spiritual clearance over our lives and over a region? First, we need to pray and research the spiritual history of our personal life and the region we are going into. We need an extensive background check. Clearing generational curses and sins is very important. We do not know everything that happened in the generations before us or in a region. Murders, wars, idolatry, the occult, sexual sins, and satanic rituals and dedications are some of the major strongholds that give the enemy a legal right to operate in our lives and regions.

This clearance is done by first going into the courts of heaven to find out the accusations and legal holds the enemy has over a region or people. What are the gates that he and his children have been possessing and through which they are perpetuating evil in that region?

For us to do a spiritual cleansing over an area, we need to research the spiritual, political, and social archives of that region or nation. To do this will require some heavy duty research both in the natural and in the spiritual. Everybody is not called to do this.

We need to go back in time and find out what and when was the first ungodly act that opened the door for the enemy to receive a foothold over that region. When was the first murder? When was the first covenant that was broken? When was the first war that took place in that area? Who started the idol or occultic worship? Which god or idol or spirit is being worshipped as a god. When and how did they all start?

Are there any demonic altars in operation? Are there any demonic or ungodly covenants in operation? These are some of the questions that need to be asked and answered. The good news is that we have Google to help us find some of these answers. More than that, we have the most powerful Search Engine God has made available, which is the Holy Spirit. The Bible says that He searches all things (1 Corinthians 2:10).

Who were the political leaders that ruled over that region and what were they like? Were they righteous, unrighteous, wicked, etc.? Were there any treasons, betrayals, adulteries, and were there any child or human sacrifices done? Are any demonic altars in operation at present? If we do not identify and cancel the legal rights of the demonic forces ruling in a region, whatever we do there will only last a matter of time. It will not stick or remain; the enemy will come and destroy it, sometimes using the same sin pattern that has been committed in that region for centuries.

There are specific people in the body of Christ who have a prophetic gifting to identify the gates of hell that are operating in a particular region. They have the skills and gifts in the Spirit to go back in time to identify, locate, and destroy these strongholds and cancel their legal rights, both in the courts of heaven and in the natural.

So far, I have met and know only one person who is actually doing this in different nations. They have taken teams and others with them to train and equip them because this task is not going to be accomplished by one individual. We need to take the entire planet back from the enemy. What gives Satan the right to continue his operation is the sins and wickedness that have been committed in a region.

That is why, though the enemy has been defeated by Jesus on the cross, he has been acting like nothing is wrong. What gives him the power to continue is these strongholds and gates that have been in operation on the earth for centuries. Jesus did His part in defeating the enemy; the rest is left for us to do.

Jesus said in John 12:31, "Now is the judgment of this world; now the ruler of this world will be cast out." The enemy's hold over this world was broken, but we have not been able to enforce that judgement until now (John 16:8-11).

That is why the Bible says He has been waiting for His enemies to be brought to His footstool (Hebrews 10:13). Jesus judged both the world and the enemy when He was on the earth (John 12:31; 16:8-11). They have no legal right to continue what they are doing, but they won't give up without a fight.

It is the same with salvation and forgiveness. Jesus died for the sins of the whole world, but not everyone is saved because they don't know their sins were forgiven by God through the cross. The same with the enemy; he has been disarmed, but what he has set in motion in the nations of the world is still there, and people continue to worship and serve him and his kingdom.

> Having disarmed principalities and powers, He made a public spectacle of them, triumphing over them in it. (Colossians 2:15)

In order for us to take back a region for God, this spiritual cleansing must be done first individually, and then region by region, city by city, and nation by nation until the whole planet is cleansed, every gate taken back and every demonic stronghold nullified and revoked. This is the real assignment of the Ekklesia in a region.

Legal Jurisdiction

What gives the enemy legal right to operate in our lives and in any region is the sins and wickedness of the people. Land is either defiled or preserved by the people. Below are some examples of wickedness that defile the land and give the enemy a legal foothold.

What gives the enemy spiritual jurisdiction over a region? Following are some of the actions, systems, places, objects, and people that could give the enemy a foothold to operate in a region.

Actions

Some of these are bloodshed, sexual sins, covenant breakings, the occult, idol worship, demonic covenants, curses, satanic rituals and sacrifices, political, social, business, and spiritual leaders and their headquarters, and decrees and proclamations by prominent people.

Systems

Some of these are various religions, their centers and headquarters, political systems and parties, governments, businesses, gods and goddesses, education systems, media, demonic laws and legislations, covens, and religious holidays.

Places

These can be specific buildings, shrines, altars, historic and cultural sights and locations, specific arts, tourist and holy sites, temples and land that have been dedicated to Satan, demonic altars, satanic churches and religious centers, ruins of historic empires, kingdoms and palaces, and even graveyards.

Objects

Some of these are monuments, statues, charms, omens, artifacts, idols, cursed objects, and even animals.

People

Some examples of these are temple priests, witches and warlocks, and political and religious leaders.

These are all potential gates of the enemy that give him the legal right to operate in a region. This is what is keeping the enemy and his kingdom operational on the earth.

Every inch of land and territory (both physical and spiritual) must be reclaimed and taken back from the enemy. The legal rights must be identified and destroyed. That is what God told Joshua when he possessed the promised land. When we read about their military and

THE PROCESS OF BECOMING A KINGDOM NATION—PART 1

spiritual operation, we will get an idea of the strategy we need to use to restore nations back to God.

We can't kill people as they did. But there will come a time when the unrepented, rebellious, and the wicked seeds of the enemy will be destroyed from this planet. That is what we read in the parable that Jesus shared about the wheat and the tares in Matthew 13. The wheat is the seed of the righteous, and the tares are the seeds of the wicked one. First, the tares will be gathered and put in fire; that is their end.

This is the reason the first responsibility of the Ekklesia in a region is to identify, locate, and destroy the gates of the enemy in that region. Then only can we inherit this earth as Jesus said in Matthew 5:5. We do not take it by our own might and power, in fact, a lot of meekness, patience, and wisdom is required to take back what the enemy stole from us. Jesus is our example; how He died on the cross and humbled Himself is the best example He gave for us to follow.

Again, please note that what Jesus is telling the Ekklesia about what we should do and how we should function are not new concepts. All of them, God already told to the people of Israel in the Old Testament. The nation of Israel and the nation of the Ekklesia both have the same purpose.

God told Abraham that his descendants will possess the gates of their enemies.

> Blessing I will bless you, and multiplying I will multiply your descendants as the stars of the heaven and as the sand which *is* on the seashore; and your descendants shall possess the gate of their enemies. (Genesis 22:17)

> And they blessed Rebekah and said to her: "Our sister, *may* you *become the mother of* thousands of ten thousands; and

may your descendants possess the gates of those who hate them." (Genesis 24:60)

And I also say to you that you are Peter, and on this rock I will build My church, and the gates of Hades shall not prevail against it. (Matthew 16:18)

Once we repossess the gates and destroy the operation of the kingdom of darkness, we need to put systems in place to guard and secure it for a thousand generations. This is a monumental task. Otherwise, what happened to Solomon will happen to us. David established the kingdom and passed it on to Solomon, but it did not last a generation. Don't let that happen to you.

Once we receive the spiritual security clearance, we need to move on to the next phase, which is the ministry of reconciliation or solving social, racial, and natural problems that exist among people. We need to identify what specific ways the people were affected by the spiritual oppression that was ruling over that area, and in which ways the enemy kingdom manifested its agenda among people. We need to address and solve these issues. This will differ from region to region. First, we must start with reconciling relationships. That is the next process.

Chapter 6

The Process of Becoming a Kingdom Nation—Part 2

> Ask of Me, and I will give You the nations for Your inheritance, and the ends of the earth for Your possession. (Psalm 2:8)

We are discussing the process of becoming a kingdom nation. In the previous chapter, I mentioned the first part, and in this chapter, we are going to discuss the rest of them.

2. Solving Social and Natural Problems

The second time Jesus mentioned the church was in the context of solving social or judicial problems between people. He said that when two people had issues they could not solve, they needed to go to the Ekklesia (or church) to get the right help.

> Moreover if your brother sins against you, go and tell him his fault between you and him alone. If he hears you, you have gained your brother. But if he will not hear, take with you one or two more, that 'by the mouth of two or three

witnesses every word may be established.' And if he refuses to hear them, tell it to the church. But if he refuses even to hear the church, let him be to you like a heathen and a tax collector. (Matthew 18:15–17)

Every local Ekklesia should have a judicial system set in place to solve the social issues between believers. When a person has an offense against another, and they cannot find a solution by themselves, they are to bring it before the Ekklesia to solve it. Jesus did not say that when two people had problems, they should go to church and worship. No, they are to *tell it to the* Ekklesia *to find the solution.*

If the church was a building, could we tell our problems to it? Of course not! But the church is not a building; it is a group of people. And if the person refuses to *hear the church* (the Ekklesia), they are to be to you like a heathen and a tax collector. It's as if they never received Christ.

The kingdom nation should have its own judicial system in place to solve the issues that arise between people. When two people have problems they cannot solve, Jesus did not say that they should go to the court system of the world, but to the church—a group of people appointed by God to administer His kingdom. Even Paul admonished the Corinthian church to not go to a court of law against another believer. He asked the church to solve the issue.

> Dare any of you, having a matter against another, go to law before the unrighteous, and not before the saints? *Do you not know that the saints will judge the world?* And if the world will be judged by you, are you unworthy to judge the smallest matters? Do you not know that we shall judge angels? *How much more, things that pertain to this life?* (1 Corinthians 6:1–3)

When do you think we will be judging the world and angels? Years ago, I was taught that we are going to heaven to sing hallelujah. But

THE PROCESS OF BECOMING A KINGDOM NATION—PART 2

that is not correct. Paul says that we are going to judge the world and angels, so how much more should we be able to judge things that pertain to this life now? When the Israelites had a judicial, social, or spiritual problem, they brought it before their elders. They did not go to a court of a gentile or an unbeliever to get help. That is the way the modern-day church is supposed to function.

In the Old Testament, Moses appointed seventy elders to solve problems for the congregation of Israel. When people had issues they could not solve, they brought the matter to those elders.

Jesus implied that the same principle needs to be followed in the Ekklesia.

Elders administered the early church. We do not see any church that was led by one pastor in the entire New Testament. When we think of the church, we need to think of it as a governing body. If we are not governing anything, then we are not functioning as a church.

The Ekklesia should have its own legal and judicial body in every town, who can serve justice to the kingdom nation citizens. I share more about this in the final chapter.

This is also an Old Covenant principle that Moses implemented to solve the problems among the people. They appointed elders to judge between people.

> Moreover you shall select from all the people able men, such as fear God, men of truth, hating covetousness; and place *such* over them *to be* rulers of thousands, rulers of hundreds, rulers of fifties, and rulers of tens. And let them judge the people at all times. Then it will be *that* every great matter they shall bring to you, but every small matter they themselves shall judge. So it will be easier for you, for they will bear *the burden* with you. If you do this thing, and God *so*

commands you, then you will be able to endure, and all this people will also go to their place in peace. (Exodus 18:21-23)

So the LORD said to Moses: "Gather to Me seventy men of the elders of Israel, whom you know to be the elders of the people and officers over them; bring them to the tabernacle of meeting, that they may stand there with you. Then I will come down and talk with you there. I will take of the Spirit that *is* upon you and will put *the same* upon them; and they shall bear the burden of the people with you, that you may not bear *it* yourself alone. (Numbers 11:16-17)

We see the apostle applying the same principles in the epistles regarding the Ekklesia.

Once we solve the social and natural problems among the people, races, and cultures, and become citizens of God's kingdom, we can move on to the next phase of the function of the Ekklesia—to become a kingdom nation.

3. Becoming a Kingdom Nation

Some people think the concept of the church did not begin until Jesus mentioned it in Matthew 16. That is not true. The church has been on this earth ever since the kingdom of God began to operate. Every kingdom or nation on this earth had a *church* or Ekklesia that administered its policies and rules. Without a church, a kingdom cannot operate—and without a kingdom, a church will not survive.

I will prove that to you from the Scriptures, in the following pages. The concept of the church was revealed in the Bible and throughout history, in both the political and spiritual sense, long before the New Testament church began. If anyone says they live in the kingdom but

THE PROCESS OF BECOMING A KINGDOM NATION—PART 2

don't want to be part of an Ekklesia, it is because they lack a true understanding of a kingdom and how it operates.

> This is he, that was *in the church in the wilderness* with the angel which spake to him in the mount Sina, and with our fathers: who received the lively oracles to give unto us. (Acts 7:38, KJV)

In this verse, Stephen uses the word Ekklesia to describe the people of Israel while they were in the wilderness. From this we understand that what might have come to the disciples' hearts when Jesus mentioned the word *Ekklesia* was a picture of the people of Israel in the wilderness. The same Greek word for *church* is used in the above verse to describe them.

What was significant about the people of Israel in the wilderness? What did they do, and how did they function as God's Ekklesia, the called-out ones? They were called out from Egypt to become a kingdom of priests and a holy nation.

If we study their lives, and the ways God dealt with them—what He did through them, how they functioned as a nation, and how they handled their internal problems—we will get somewhat of an understanding of the Ekklesia in the New Testament. Paul said that everything they went through was for our example (1 Corinthians 10:6, 11).

The Israelites were *called out* from Egypt by God to be a special kingdom, or a nation of kings and priests (Exodus 19:6), through whom He would accomplish His purpose on earth. The church today is also the called-out ones, a royal priesthood, and a holy nation (1 Peter 2:9).

When Israel rebelled against God, they went into captivity in Babylon. God brought them out of Babylon and established them as

THE BIRTHING OF A KINGDOM NATION

a nation again. Now God is following the same pattern by calling His people out of Egypt (religion) and Babylon (this world's system) to form the kingdom nation.

They were in the process of becoming a kingdom nation. God called them out of Egypt to become a nation, not a choir. While they were in the wilderness, He was implementing each component they would need, so that when they reached the promised land, they would be ready to function as a kingdom nation.

When we think of the church today, we should think of it as a nation ruled by a King. Too many people believe that we don't belong here on earth, and they are waiting to fly away. But that wasn't the way the Israelites (Old Testament Ekklesia) thought or functioned.

Imagine a nation that has been divided into millions of pieces. How effective can that nation be? That is what happened to the body of Christ. Even though we are one body, we have been divided into millions of pieces, so that even a small enemy can easily conquer a local church. This needs to change, and it is about to change.

A nation could be divided into states or provinces under one centralized governing authority and still function well. Unfortunately, the Spirit-filled body of Christ does not have the necessary unity and centralized governing system to accomplish that task. This is our biggest weakness.

If we look at the people of Israel, they were twelve tribes composed of millions of people with various gifts, talents, and callings; but they functioned as *one* nation under God. People have divided the body of Christ into pieces for personal gain, selfish ambition, or by the deception of the enemy. This must change.

What were the people of Israel doing in the wilderness? They were not coming together once a week to sing some songs and hear

THE PROCESS OF BECOMING A KINGDOM NATION—PART 2

Moses preach. They were in the process of becoming a nation and a kingdom. Through Moses, God implemented everything a nation was supposed to have.

They had their own economy, education system, agriculture, judicial system, etc. There was a spiritual aspect as well. God used Moses to establish them as a nation and institute the components mentioned above and others as well. The church is a nation. It needs to have all the components a nation has, so it can represent its King and His kingdom.

The reason the church is not able to function as a nation or a kingdom yet is because we have not completed our wilderness journey. Most perish in the wilderness without inheriting their promises or fulfilling their destinies. We still have a wilderness or Egyptian mindset.

After writing this, it seems to me that the majority of the church is not even in the wilderness yet. They are still in Egypt or in Babylon, serving another king and building another kingdom with their sweat and blood. Lord have mercy!

If you are still looking for miracles to survive, and trying to experience God based on feelings or seeing something, know that you are still in the wilderness. That is how the Israelites lived. You live in today's promised land by faith and produce what you need.

Adam was not living by miracles in the garden. There was a constant supply of provision and resources there. He did not lack anything he needed to fulfill his God-given assignment. God was his Source.

God wanted the Israelites to be a kingdom governed by Him (Exodus 19:6). He wanted to show the whole world His original plan and purpose for mankind. He wanted them to be a light to the gentiles. When they saw that light, He expected them to come to Him through Israel. That is the same plan He has for the church.

THE BIRTHING OF A KINGDOM NATION

We have limited the church to a spiritual or religious entity doing spiritual things or charitable works. That is far from the truth. God is doing a new thing in His church; He is bringing it back to its original intent.

As we study the early Ekklesia, we will see how they functioned as a nation or a kingdom. They had an economy; that is why there was no one in the church who had an unmet need. They did not go to the gentiles for help or for a loan. I explain this in my book *Kingdom Secrets to Restoring Nations Back to God*.

The nation of Israel was established by God through twelve men, the sons of Jacob. When they moved to Egypt, they were only seventy people in total (Exodus 1:5). They began to multiply and became a mighty nation. When they failed to fulfill the purpose of God, He chose another twelve men—the apostles of Jesus—to start another nation.

Jesus followed the same principle to start this new nation called the Ekklesia. This time, the nation was not limited to a particular geographic area. He started with twelve apostles, and then selected seventy people and sent them out to the cities and towns He was going to visit (Luke 10:1). Why do we see the numbers twelve and seventy in both cases?

Twelve is the number of government, or the kingdom. To begin a nation, the minimum number of people required was seventy; the church is supposed to function as a nation. Now we are in that process of becoming one. God will destroy every *denomination* that was started by men and brought His people under much *condemnation*. This caused the church to become an *abomination* to the people of this world. Let's turn and go back to our original *destination,* which is to become a *kingdom nation*.

THE PROCESS OF BECOMING A KINGDOM NATION—PART 2

Once we become a kingdom nation, we can start influencing the world and the culture we live in. We will have something to show to the world. Then, we can send ambassadors (missionaries) and diplomats to other nations, and we can move on to the next phase of becoming a political force for God and His kingdom. Until then, we should not get involved in the politics of any nation because we don't have the proper foundation to provide the support and system that we need to go into the world.

4. Becoming a Political or Legal Assembly

When you read Acts 19:23–41, you will see that the word Ekklesia appears three times. It describes a lawful political gathering in each case (Acts 19:32, 39, 41), but it is translated "church" elsewhere. In these verses, it is translated "assembly."

> If there is anything further you want to bring up, it must be settled in a legal assembly. (Acts 19:39, NIV)

When Paul and his team came to Ephesus preaching the gospel of the kingdom, the idol makers were worried about their trade and profit, so they brought accusations against Paul and his team for trying to put them out of business. The matter was brought to the city officials, and they came together to deliberate and make a decision. Such gatherings of city officials or rulers, in those days, were called an *Ekklesia*.

In the kingdom nation, each city needs to have a functioning Ekklesia. That is why the churches in the New Testament were not called by any name or by the names of preachers. It was just called the church, or the Ekklesia, of Rome or Corinth or Ephesus, etc. It meant the governing body of Rome or Corinth or Ephesus.

Each time Jesus mentioned the Ekklesia, He referred to a governing body, not a place of worship or a building. He spoke of a group of

THE BIRTHING OF A KINGDOM NATION

people who were assigned to exercise authority to solve problems both in the *spiritual* and in the *natural* world. In the political world of those days, the Ekklesia was a group of people who were called out—or selected—from the general public to govern the affairs of the kingdom or nation.

The disciples knew that every king had an Ekklesia in his kingdom, that governed his affairs. That's why they kept questioning Jesus as to when He was going to set up His kingdom on the earth. They wanted to sit and rule with Him (Matthew 20:21, Acts 1:6), and function as an Ekklesia.

When we read the gospel of Matthew, we notice that it was after Jesus said He would build His Ekklesia that the mother of James and John came requesting that her sons sit on His right and His left in His kingdom (Mat- thew 20:20–21). They wanted to be part of His governing body, but they only understood the natural aspect of the term. That's what they were familiar with at that time. The spiritual revelation of His kingdom, or Ekklesia, came to them later.

What I like about those guys is that at least they had a kingdom mindset. They wanted to rule with Him. They didn't come to tell Jesus they wanted to conduct an all-night singing party with smoke machines and coffee and donuts for Him when He establishes His kingdom.

When we think of the church, we need to think about it in all seven of the contexts I am mentioning here: a kingdom, a governing body, a nation, and a legal assembly, and the rest I share below. Only then will we have a complete picture of how a local Ekklesia is supposed to function. The bottom line is that in all of its contexts, it is a *governing* body.

Compare this with how the *church* functions and operates in our day. What do we need to do to bring the church back to what Jesus meant it to be? Take some time and think about that, and see if you can come up with some action steps.

THE PROCESS OF BECOMING A KINGDOM NATION—PART 2

Once the Ekklesia is formed as a nation, the next step is to become a political force on earth for God and His kingdom. Many Christians now are trying to enter politics and bring changes in their nations. Most fail because they do not have the support of the kingdom nation, or the Ekklesia. They are there on their own, trying to face the enemy by themselves, and most of the time, they get beaten and eaten by the enemy. They do not have the spiritual security clearance and support they need.

Some are trying with a great zeal and passion to take over Babylon and turn it into a Christian nation. That is the wrong spirit and the wrong motive. We are not here to take over Babylon. Babylon must fall. I will share more about this later in the Government of God chapters.

This shouldn't happen. We can only send ambassadors to foreign nations after we become a nation. Joseph and Moses were sent to Egypt by God. They did not take over those nations or their governments. The same thing happened to Daniel. He reached Babylon because of the captivity.

God wanted them to be lights to the gentiles, but that would not have happened on their own. He had to orchestrate it to get them where He needed them to be; in these cases, through slavery and captivity. It was the same with Esther in Persia. She wouldn't have signed up on her own to become the next queen. God needed to get her there.

Once the nation of Israel was established, they became a political force in the region and in the world at large. They traded with other nations. They did not borrow but lent to many nations. Because of the governmental calling upon my life, I am drawn to politics and affairs of governments.

One day, I was traveling in a taxi through the city of New Delhi, the capital of India. There is a particular area of every capital city where all the embassies are located. On this particular day, I was driving through that region, and as I was passing by different embassies, I noticed something that my eyes couldn't believe. In passing, I read something written on a wall: The Embassy of the Apostolic Church of the Holy See. I couldn't believe what I was reading. I thought I was dreaming or seeing a vision.

I wondered who started this apostolic church in the capital city of India, among all these embassies. I wanted to tell the driver to turn around and go back, but I did not. I wanted to go and check it out to see if what I saw was real. Though I did not fully understand what I saw that day, it stayed in my memory. I thought it was a church that someone started for all the ambassadors from different nations, but it was not a church as we think of it.

Fifteen years later, the Lord opened a door for me to become a peace Ambassador of the United Nations, which prompted me to look at the website of the Vatican City and the Roman Catholic Church. From the information I gathered, I found out that what I saw in New Delhi that day was the Embassy of the Catholic Church and Vatican City. They have their embassies all over the world.

The kingdom nation needs ambassadors and diplomatic centers represented in every nation. We will need our own seat in the United Nations, like every other nation, because we will be the ones providing solutions to the problems other nations are facing. We are supposed to be the light of this world.

Only after we are established as a kingdom nation, should we send out ambassadors, apostles, and missionaries to different nations to represent our King and His kingdom. Then there will be value and worth ascribed to the person being sent. They won't be going on their own and operating at their own risk; they will be the sent ones—fully supported and covered by the kingdom nation.

5. The Process of Dominion

If you have been around this ministry or read any of the previous books, you will know the dominion mandate very well because that is the purpose for which God created mankind. He didn't change His mind concerning our purpose because Adam fell. Our purpose remains the same throughout all generations.

What I did not understand for a long time is that what God told Adam to do, and why He established the nation of Israel and the church, are all for one and the same reason. All three have the same purpose. We thought there was no relationship or connection between Eden, Israel, and the church, but that is incorrect.

> Then God said, "Let Us make man in Our image, according to Our likeness; let them have dominion over the fish of the sea, over the birds of the air, and over the cattle, over all the earth and over every creeping thing that creeps on the earth." (Genesis 1:26)

Why would God create mankind and tell them to have dominion? Dominion simply means to rule. He wanted them to rule the earth. Why would God tell Adam to take dominion over the fish of the sea, birds of the air, and other creatures?

It is because of what happened to the earth and what was going on spiritually in the unseen background before Adam arrived. God told them to have dominion over every aspect of creation. Remember that the first responsibility of the Ekklesia is to obtain spiritual clearance, or to create a spiritual defense over the earth so there is no chance for any spiritual intruder to do anything contrary to God and His will on the earth.

God wanted Adam to protect and defend the earth from any demonic forces entering or establishing anything here. I recommend you read *The Gospel of the Kingdom* where I explain this in detail, including the pre-Adamic history of the earth.

Lucifer had access to this earth before the creation of Adam, but because he is a spiritual being, he had no right to do anything on the earth. It was to humans that God gave the right to rule this planet. If Lucifer was to obtain the legal right to establish his kingdom on the earth, he would have to receive it from Adam.

The only way to steal that right from Adam was if Lucifer could deceive him by lying. Jesus said that one of the things the devil does when he comes is "steal" (John 10:10). He is the father of all lies.

If any spirit beings want to do anything legal on the earth, they are required to have a physical body. Somebody needed to provide Satan a body to allow him to come to the garden and do anything there. Those creatures mentioned in Genesis 1:26 were the ones with physical bodies. They were the potential gates. Adam and Eve wouldn't give their bodies to the enemy.

Satan chose the serpent because it was more cunning than any other creature the Lord God had created. By telling Adam to take dominion over those creatures, God was warning and preparing him to not allow any usurpations or rebellion in the garden from any of the creatures.

If Adam noticed any unusual activities or heard any voices speaking contrary to what God had told him, his responsibility was to subdue and silence them, and keep everything in alignment with God and His kingdom.

It was to Adam that God gave the complete jurisdiction of the earth. Whatever he did affected the entire earth and all of creation. "Out of the ground the Lord God formed every beast of the field and every bird of the air, and brought *them* to Adam to see what he would call them. And **whatever Adam** called each living creature, that *was* its name." (Genesis 2:19)

God told Abraham that whoever blesses him will be blessed and whoever curses him will be cursed. God wants to bless all the families of the earth through him. That is dominion.

The jurisdiction related to the earth realm has been committed to humans. Jesus told the church the same thing in Matthew 16:19, "And I will give you the keys of the Kingdom of Heaven. **Whatever you** forbid on earth will be forbidden in heaven, and **whatever you** permit on earth will be permitted in heaven." (NLT)

The Ekklesia holds the keys of governance over the entire earth. We have the right to permit or not to permit what happens here. The reason it is not happening practically is because of the division among the body of Christ. When we are united in the purpose of building God's kingdom on earth, nothing will be impossible for us. All of creation will remain subject to us.

When the sons of God manifest the kingdom nation, they will set in motion the healing and restoration of the whole creation. I share in a later chapter how God will heal the nations, as we read in Revelation 22:2.

There is a specific reason Jesus did not go around and conduct praise and worship services with the disciples. He knew the blueprint, and He followed the step-by-step process of building His Ekklesia. He cannot put the cart before the horse. We did not understand the blueprint or God's purpose, so we just went ahead with whatever worked for us.

6. The Process of Devotion

The religious church has been good in this area. Devotion involves ministering to the Lord in songs, praise, thanksgiving, and teaching the word. In Acts, we read this about the believers:

Then those who gladly received his word were baptized; and that day about three thousand souls were added *to them*. And they continued steadfastly in the apostles' doctrine and fellowship, in the breaking of bread, and in prayers. (Acts 2:41-42)

And daily in the temple, and in every house, they did not cease teaching and preaching Jesus *as* the Christ. (Acts 5:42)

The purpose of the apostles' doctrine is to equip each believer to discover and fulfill their kingdom assignment, and to present them perfect before Christ our King. This is one of the main reasons we gather in a building or a place.

But we have made gathering the most important thing and neglected the above-mentioned functions. As a result, we became a religious or social entity. I am not going to spend much time explaining this; we are all familiar with this function because we have been experiencing this in the church all along.

7. The Process of Functioning as a Body or Family

In Paul's writing, he compares the Ekklesia to a human body. Though we are many members, we are all supposed to function as one body with each member having a unique place and a specific role that no other member can fill.

For example, the function of our eyes, our ears cannot fulfill, regardless of how hard they try.

But now God has set the members, each one of them, in the body just as He pleased. (1 Corinthians 12:18) But now indeed *there are* many members, yet one body. (1 Corinthians 12:20)

THE PROCESS OF BECOMING A KINGDOM NATION—PART 2

Instead of functioning as one body, people have isolated themselves based on gifts and built their own empires. Imagine one part of our body trying to do the job of the whole body; it won't work, it will malfunction. That is what is happening to the body of Christ everywhere.

The concept of a body is to emphasize the importance of relationship and fellowship, and to show that we are all connected to one another. We cannot focus just on relationship by neglecting the other components or processes.

The Divine Blueprint

There is a divine progression in the order of how the word Ekklesia is defined in the above seven contexts or processes. In other words, there is a blueprint revealed that every local Ekklesia, or the body of Christ in a country, should follow. That is how the kingdom of God will manifest in a region. What do I mean by that?

The first context is the kingdom—that's the purpose of the Ekklesia. Jesus started the Ekklesia to administer His kingdom and to withstand and destroy the operation of the gates of hell. But an Ekklesia does not stop there. That just solves the spiritual problem. Once we confront and dispossess the gates of hell in a community, we move on to the next level.

The next level is solving social and judicial issues, the natural problems of the people and community. And we don't stop there either. We need to go to the next level of nation-building, just like the people of Israel did in the wilderness as an Ekklesia of God. We need to become a functioning kingdom nation of kings and priests.

The Israelites were preparing to establish themselves as a nation, once they arrived in the promised land. They had everything that any other nation had, and likewise, the Ekklesia in a city should develop and have everything a nation has. We are supposed to function as a nation within every country. They did not build synagogues in every village. The synagogue system came later when they lost their kingdom purpose and became a religious entity.

Once we have everything a nation has, we move to the next level, which is to become a political force in our nation, just like we saw the word Ekklesia used in the fourth context above. Only when an Ekklesia completes these seven levels, or stages, can it begin to establish God's kingdom on earth. Then we will see God's will established in every sphere of society, as it is in heaven.

There is only one religious denominational church that has reached all these seven levels on the earth today, but their doctrines are messed up, so they cannot establish God's kingdom. If their doctrines were sound, they would have been the greatest force for God because they have branches in almost every nation on earth; and they are a political force.

We see this same pattern in the Bible from the very beginning. God started with the kingdom in Genesis 1:26 by telling mankind to exercise dominion on this planet for Him; then eventually, that one man would become a nation, and nations on the earth would be serving God. Note the first promise God gave to Abraham was that he would become a great nation.

When the Israelites reached the promised land, they became a political force for God and His kingdom. That is our destination also as an Ekklesia of God. In the book of Revelation, we see that people from every nation and tongue will join together and become part of God's kingdom, and we will become a political force for Him on the earth. Jesus is and will be our King. He will lead us to battle against the armies of the kingdom of darkness.

THE PROCESS OF BECOMING A KINGDOM NATION—PART 2

God gave me this revelation when I was in Liberia for a kingdom assignment. One morning, I woke up with a dream. In the dream, I saw or heard, "Moses is dead," and then I saw Joshua preaching and training people about the tactics and practical steps to possess the land.

Globally, the Ekklesia of God is still in the wilderness stage (many are still in Egypt), and we are in the process of entering the promised land to possess the earth for the kingdom. The "Moses generation" is coming to a close, and God is raising up a "Joshua generation" to accomplish this task. They will establish the *nation* of God in every country.

Chapter 7

Discovering the Lost Father

And this is eternal life, that they may know You, the only true God, and Jesus Christ whom You have sent. (John 17:3)

There are only three major problems on this planet. All other problems are connected and will be solved once we solve these three. The first is that people do not know who the real God of the Bible is (this includes Christians). I spent the first forty years of my life as a Christian serving a religious spirit. I thought I was serving God. God is the most misunderstood and misrepresented Person on the earth.

The second major problem is that people do not know their purpose, as I mentioned earlier. And the third is that things that happened to us, from the time of conception till now, have created a distorted and defective view of ourselves, God, others, and the world around us.

When we solve these three problems, every other problem will be solved on its own. Before we can restore anything outside, we first need to be restored inside. To be restored inside, we first need to discover the Father we lost in the garden, which Jesus came to reveal in the Gospels. What Jesus did not do, or say, to an individual, God will not do, or say, to an individual.

The Character of the Father

The Father we see in the Old Covenant is not the true nature and character of God. Do you know that we can create or make a god on our own? People have made millions of gods and goddesses since the fall of Adam. And they continue to do so.

As we are learning about the kingdom nation, it is important to learn the character and nature of the King of the kingdom, or the nation. If we do not understand His heart toward us, then our perception of ourselves and the world around us will also be distorted.

Before we can function as a kingdom nation, it is important that all father wounds (both natural and spiritual) in our heart and soul are healed, and we have the correct perception and understanding of God and His nature. We all need to become one with Him, and in Him, 24/7, not just have a spiritual experience on a Sunday morning for two hours and then go on with our lives.

Statistics say the number one reason children misbehave and end up in bad company is because of the absence of a father in their life, or in their family. The major reason most people don't reach their potential, or fulfill their destiny, is because they did not receive what they needed from their father, or worse, because of the wounds and abuse they experienced from their father.

Why do young people look up to evil men and consider them their heroes or role models, and join notorious gangs around the world? They are looking for a father figure. They are trying to fill a vacuum that is in their soul. Life without a father is filled with chaos, disorder, and dysfunction.

Whether you believe it or not, your heart and soul are longing for a father. Our prisons are filled with men and women, and if we listen to their stories, we find that the majority will go back to the root of a bad experience they had with their father while growing up. The fruit they are bearing now is rooted in an absentee or abusive father. Our nursing and old-age homes are filled with people who are still looking for their Daddy.

When you discover the kingdom of God, your spirit will find its home and its purpose. When you discover your heavenly Father, you will find your true identity. The number one crisis of our time is the identity crisis, and the number one theft is stealing someone's identity. The enemy of old has always been good at stealing people's identity.

God doesn't define your identity, destiny, and value based on what happened to you, where you are from, or what you did or did not do. Our identity, purpose, value, and worth must be re-established apart from the culture we grew up in, our gender, what happened to us, the color of our skin, our nationality, education, titles, outward looks, what we do, what we possess, or to whom we are connected.

Most of us spend the majority of our time regretting what happened to us in the past, or worrying about the future that is not here yet, and we miss the present. God is always good, but only a few people truly believe that in their heart. They say it with their mouth, but in their heart they have conflicting opinions of Him. On Sunday morning, they will shout that He is good, but on Monday morning, they will doubt His goodness.

Misunderstood Father

God is the most misunderstood Person in the universe. The kingdom of God is the most lost doctrine of the Bible. And all religions and denominations came into existence because of that misconception. The Bible says that God is love, but most people don't experience or receive His love. They hate Him or are angry at Him because they do not believe that He really loves them.

They read in the Bible that God is love, but their heart feels like a parched and dry land, waiting for the rain. Their hearts are deprived of love because they never experienced what true love is. If God is love, then why are most people not experiencing His love?

When it comes to the church, people have different opinions of God. They think their God is mean and evil, and they don't know how to reconcile what happened in the Old Testament with the Jesus they see in the New Testament. The Father they see in the Old Testament is mean, strict, angry, and killing people and burning cities. If God is love, how can that be an expression of love?

The body of Christ is divided into pieces based on which line of the Bible each group believes. Then they fight with each other, using those "lines" to attack one another, thinking they are superior or holier than the group on the other side of the road. When the world sees that in us, they mock us and make fun of us. We have miserably failed to manifest the Father to the world.

We have made this earth almost uninhabitable for humans, and we are not willing to accept the responsibility for the mess we created. Instead, we are waiting to escape and go to heaven. How will we love each other and have unity among us in heaven if we can't get along with each other inside the same house on the earth? Does God have separate places in heaven for believers from different denominations? I don't think so.

All of the denominations and groupism that we have in the body of Christ came because of the misunderstanding we have of the Father. We misunderstood Him, His purpose, His original intention, His nature, His character, and His love.

DISCOVERING THE LOST FATHER

Something happened to our perception of God since the fall of Adam, which is the root issue of every other problem and mess we see out there. We are going to explore what happened to us and how can we return to the heavenly Father we lost. Jesus came to show us the way to the Father.

When I was a slave to a religion called Christianity, I couldn't understand the heart of God. I thought He was strict, mean, and bossy. I did not understand why He killed all the people and was angry so many times. When I came into the kingdom, I understood His heart and nature, and I came to realize that whatever happened under the Old Covenant was not His fault or intention. It was the people that brought all that evil and destruction upon themselves. He remained good and just all the time.

People ask difficult questions like, 'If God is good, or if He is love, then why does He allow evil, poverty, sickness, accidents, storms, and wars on the earth? Why doesn't He help the poor or those who are suffering?' We are going to find out that it was not God who initiated all of this evil; it was humans. God gave the right to rule the earth only to mankind, and the right to decide what needs to happen here.

God gave mankind complete jurisdiction over the earth realm. We can create different forms of government, and different kinds of religions and gods. We can create a communist form of government, and when we do that, we will experience the result of it in our nations and lives. We can create a totalitarian type of government, and we will expe- rience the result of it.

We can form a democratic or capitalistic form of government, and we will experience the results of it in our daily life. We can't blame God for the results we experience from the systems and processes we set up over us.

In the same way, the majority of the things we experience in life is based on the belief system we have in our mind. These belief systems can be formed by truth or lies. In the natural, we are free to create different forms of government and experience life based on them; in the spirit, we are free to create our own systems of belief about God. The life we experience will be based on those belief systems. We cannot blame God for that.

That is what Adam did in the beginning. He chose a life and a system that is apart from God. Since he was the first human, what he did, and what happened to him, affected the entire human race. This created a wrong impression of God the Father in the hearts and minds of people.

Adam declared independence from God and His kingdom, and decided to initiate a system based on the knowledge of good and evil to create his own god, kingdom, and destiny. This forced God to deal with mankind based on our actions, instead of dealing with us based on His goodness.

Ever since this misconception emerged in the hearts of humans about the true nature of God, we couldn't understand His love and purpose. We felt like helpless victims trying to please a God who is so distant from us that it doesn't matter what or how much we do.

Some people became smarter than others, and they began to manufacture new gods and religions to exploit and manipulate others. They required money through extortion and demanded obedience from people in order to receive favors from those gods. Everything was based on fear and fear of punishment.

As a result, millions of gods and goddesses were formed on the earth. Many stopped believing in any god at all. To end this menace, and to clear the misunderstanding we have of Him, God

Almighty did something extra ordinary. He became incarnate to manifest on the earth in human form. To change the misconceptions and misunderstanding people have of God the Father, He manifested Himself to humanity in the Person of Jesus Christ. This chapter is about discovering the Father that Jesus came to reveal.

Every other notion and understanding about God the Father, other than what we see revealed through the life of Jesus, is not valid. Jesus is the only express image of the godhead. This means that Jesus is the only authorized version of God the Father. So if you want to know who the real Father is, get to know Jesus.

God spoke and revealed Himself in the Old Testament in many ways and forms. But people couldn't understand Him because they were stuck in a system of life that was not authorized by Him. I will explain more about this.

Jesus is Immanuel, God with us, among us, and in us. Do you want to know the true and only God? Look at Jesus: His life, nature, character, attitude, and love. Look at how He dealt and related with people. Compare the concept you have of God with what Jesus did and said while He was on the earth. If it is conflicting with the concept of God you have in your heart, then this book will help you get rid of those wrong perceptions, and you can finally become one with God.

It is possible to live in the security of God's constant love, protection, and provision. God is kind, compassionate, and merciful. What happened in the Old Testament was not His fault. You are going to find out that it was man's fault all along.

When you finish reading this book, if it clears some misunderstanding you have of God, then I am happy, and my Father is happy. He is waiting for you to come home; He has many rooms in His heart for us. Each one of us has a unique place in His heart. You don't need to wander any more in life looking for love and validation. When you discover Him, you will find everything you will ever need in your life.

There are specific reasons why there are four gospels in the New Testament. Matthew is the only gospel that uses the phrase "kingdom of heaven" because it introduces the re-entry or arrival of the kingdom and the King back to earth. Mark focuses on the power of the kingdom. The focus of Luke is the administration of the kingdom. And John focuses on reintroducing and restoring our lost Father.

If we are to understand what really happened to Adam in the garden, we need to understand the two specific trees that were in the garden and what they represented. They were not just two normal trees as we think of trees. They represented two different kinds of life and how we want to live. That is why one of them was called the Tree of Life. We are going to explore them here.

Two Trees in the Garden

> And out of the ground the Lord God made every tree grow that is pleasant to the sight and good for food. The tree of life *was* also in the midst of the garden, and the tree of the knowledge of good and evil. (Genesis 2:9)

> Then the serpent said to the woman, "You will not surely die. For God knows that in the day you eat of it your eyes will be opened, and you will be like God, knowing good and evil." (Genesis 3:4-5)

> So when the woman saw that the tree *was* good for food, that it *was* pleasant to the eyes, and a tree desirable to make *one* wise, she took of its fruit and ate. She also gave to her

husband with her, and he ate. Then the eyes of both of them were opened, and they knew that they *were* naked; and they sewed fig leaves together and made themselves coverings. (Genesis 3:6-7)

Those two trees represented two systems of life. The Tree of Life represented a life that comes from God based on His unconditional love toward us. God is the Source of that life. He becomes the Source of our joy, the reason for our existence, and everything else. Apart from Him, there is no life or reason to live.

When Adam ate from the Tree of the Knowledge of Good and Evil, it changed his perception of God because it initiated a system or knowledge that was apart from God. He began to feel that God loves and accepts him based on his works or performance. He became the god. He became self-conscious instead of God-conscious. Fear came into his life, and he lost the confidence to face God.

This happened because Adam lost the spirit of sonship, and a spirit of bondage ruled by fear came into his life. An orphan spirit came into him, and he felt lonely and rejected. He lost the ability to understand the true nature of God. When we eat from the Tree of the Knowledge of Good and Evil, it is impossible to know the true nature and character of God. It will be distorted.

Two kinds of Life

Thus far, we have only known God through the system of the knowledge of good and evil. That is not the true God, and that is not the right perception of Him. Jesus came to reveal the Father. He said that he who has seen Him has seen the Father.

The only God this world has known is the God who deals with humans based on their works or performance, which was initiated by

Adam. Most people rejected Him because their works were evil. They did not think God would accept them if they came to Him. Jesus came to change the wrong perception we had of the Father. God is love.

A religious spirit was released to the earth in the garden when Adam chose to activate a life that is apart from God, and then tried to be like God, or receive His love and acceptance based on behavior modification or performance. The more we try to be good and please God under this system, the harder we fail and fall. The foundation of every religion is to live according to the knowledge of good and evil. God did not start any religion; humans did.

What is the system of the knowledge of good and evil? It says that when we do good, God will accept and bless us, but when we do evil, He will reject and punish us. That is what we see happening in the Old Testament. When people did good, God blessed them, but when they did evil, He punished or judged them.

It was not God's fault. Adam activated the system of the knowledge of good and evil and put God in a predicament. Even though He is good all the time, He couldn't show His goodness to people because they believed something different. They expected His rejection and punishment. What we believe has power over us. Everything in God's kingdom works based on our belief system. That is why Jesus kept emphasizing what people believed when they came to Him.

Below are some of the results of eating from the Tree of the Knowledge of Good and Evil.

It makes us look into ourselves

We always see what's wrong with us; our nakedness, our fear, our lack, what we did in the past—instead of God.

The Bible says to look to Jesus who is the author and finisher of our faith (Hebrews 12:2).

Once Adam ate the wrong fruit, it changed his focus, and then when he looked inside, instead of seeing God and His kingdom, he started seeing his faults and deficiencies. A wrong set of eyes had been opened, just as the serpent foretold.

It changes our perception of God

God is the most misunderstood Person. His character, His nature, and His intent have been misunderstood for centuries because men have stayed under the Tree of the Knowledge of Good and Evil and continued to eat it's fruit.

It changes our perception of ourselves

Adam was a son, but once he ate the wrong fruit, he couldn't see himself as a son anymore. He saw himself as a failure, as a salve, as an orphan, as rejected, and abandoned. He couldn't come to God anymore and be real with Him. Instead, he chose to hide from Him.

It gives the devil authority over us

The devil cannot defeat us; he can only deceive us first with his lies, and then we defeat ourselves.

It changes how we see the world around us

When we live under this tree, we will love people based on their behavior and not based on their personhood. Jesus told us to love our neighbor, not based on their behavior, but as we love ourselves.

It changes how we view others and treat them

Why do we have such difficulty loving others? It is mainly because we don't love or even like ourselves.

It causes us to depend on our works

It made us "human doings" instead of "human beings." We love to perform, and we love the applause we receive from people. We began to value ourselves based on what we do and how we do it, instead of who God made us.

It produces religion

All religion came from the Tree of the Knowledge of Good and Evil. That is the root of it. All religion believes the same thing: if we do good, then God will accept us; but when we do evil, he will reject and forsake us.

It brings us under the bondage of sin

Sin was activated and came to earth by Adam eating from the wrong tree. The Tree of the Knowledge of Good and Evil is the source and representation of sin, just like the devil is the father of all lies.

The Tree of the Knowledge of Good and Evil is the father of all religion.

- Religion is man's attempt to reach God by good works or behavior.
- Religion is man trying to please God through works.

- Religion is made of rituals and practices and traditions of men, and then putting God in a box of those rituals and traditions.

It creates human gods or humanism

The promise the serpent made was, "You will be like God." This means you will be like a god but apart and separated from the true God. Appoint yourself as gods, and then do your own thing: whatever you want and whenever you want it. Have some fun!

Humanism is man placing himself as god and having nothing to do with God and His purposes. That's what has happened throughout history. Man replaced God and appointed himself as god, and then began to worship themselves and others. Super heroes and celebrities are human gods we worship and adore.

So, what we see from Genesis chapter 3 through the end of Malachi is the result or the fruit of people living according to the knowledge of good and evil. The entire old covenant was built on this system. God never wanted humans to live according to the knowledge of good and evil. He wanted them to be led by His Spirit.

The Tree of Life

The whole Bible, and our life on earth, is the story of three trees: the two that were in the garden and the cross on which Jesus hung and gave His life for us all. Trees represent life and people in the Bible. Everything in the kingdom of God has been represented by a tree in the Bible.

Trees sustain life on earth, and everything that is essential to life comes from trees and plants—even the air we breathe and all the food we eat. The meat we eat is included because animals eat their food, which is made from trees or plants.

Our ecosystem is sustained by the trees. We breathe in what trees breathe out; and they breathe in what we breathe out. Our life is connected to trees, so it's no wonder God put two trees in the garden and told us to choose which tree we want to be associated with.

Kingdom Lost

The purpose of all Jesus's teaching and preaching was to reveal God's (our Father's) heart and His kingdom to mankind. We were lost: first, we lost our relationship with God as our Father, and as a result, we lost our purpose. We have since been held as slaves by another king and his kingdom.

Sin is the system by which the enemy keeps us as his slaves and tied to his kingdom. Grace, love, and righteousness are the system through which God demonstrates His heart and kingdom toward us because He wants us to become His sons and daughters; He wants to free us from the clutches of sin and Satan. Unfortunately, religion has made us believe the opposite.

Religion made us believe that Jesus came to take us all to heaven. Neither Jesus nor the apostles ever asked anyone if they want to go to heaven when they die. I couldn't find even one verse in all four Gospels to support that theory.

Jesus never said that He is the way to heaven. He said that He is the way to the Father. Jesus came to reveal the heart of the Father and His true nature. Through the fall of Adam, mankind inherited a wrong perception of the heart and nature of God.

It was not God's fault; it was Adam who activated the harmful system of this life by eating the fruit of the tree from which God said not to eat. The fruit of the Tree of the Knowledge of Good and Evil initiated a wrong impression of God in the hearts and spirits of humans, and it activated a destructive system of life on earth.

Adam's choice of eating from the wrong tree resulted in God having to deal with men and women based on their works. When they did good, He accepted them and blessed them, and when they did evil, He punished or killed them. Actually, it was not God who did that; it was the system that Adam initiated. It is similar to the system of government we choose. We receive the consequence of the government we live under.

That is what we see throughout the Old Testament. When people did good, God blessed them. When they did evil, He punished them. It created a wrong perception of God in mankind. Instead of running to God when they need help, they started running away from Him because, to them, He seemed hard to please.

Jesus Came to Reveal the Father

To change the wrong perception that was created by the knowledge of good and evil, God decided to come down Himself to show us who He is and what is His nature looks like, and His heart toward us. That is what we see in Jesus Christ, the Son of the living God.

Jesus came to reveal the Father to us. He came to show us what the Father thinks toward us. He is God in human form. That is why the Bible says, "And the Word became flesh and dwelt among us, and we beheld His glory, the glory as of the only begotten of the Father, full of grace and truth." (John 1:14)

> No one has seen God at any time. The only begotten Son, who is in the bosom of the Father, He has declared *Him*. (John 1:18)

This verse means that no one has the right to tell us what God is like, and His heart toward us, except His only begotten Son. No prophet or scribe has that privilege or understanding. They all knew Him, or about Him, partially. But finally, we received an opportunity through His Son to know who the Father is and what His true nature is like.

That is why the verse says, "No one has seen God at any time." No one means no one. No one has the right to express what God is like except His Son who is in the bosom of the Father. That means that what Jesus did not do or say to an individual, the Father won't do or say to anyone. What Jesus won't say to humans, the Father won't say to us.

Jesus also said that He and the Father are one. He is in the Father, and the Father is in Him. He who has seen Him has seen the Father. That is a powerful statement. The whole purpose of the Gospel of John is to reveal the Father and His nature to us.

> Not that anyone has seen the Father, except He who is from God; He has seen the Father. (John 6:46) I and *My* Father are one. (John 10:30)

> Jesus said to him, "I am the way, the truth, and the life. No one comes to the Father except through Me." (John 14:6)

> If you had known Me, you would have known My Father also; and from now on you know Him and have seen Him. (John 14:7)

One of the disciples, Philip, asked Jesus to show him the Father. They wanted to know how this Father looks and what He thought of them. They all had the wrong concept and knowledge of Him, and they were tired and weary from trying to please Him. It seemed like nothing was good enough for Him.

> Philip said to Him, "Lord, show us the Father, and it is sufficient for us." (John 14:8)

DISCOVERING THE LOST FATHER

To which Jesus replied:

> "Have I been with you so long, and yet you have not known Me, Philip? He who has seen Me has seen the Father; so how can you say, 'Show us the Father'? (John 14:9)

If God is good all the time, then why do most people on earth run away from Him and want nothing to do with Him, instead of running to Him? If God is love, then why has mankind created millions of gods and goddesses and worships them instead of Him?

Jesus went on to say:

> Do you not believe that I am in the Father, and the Father in Me? The words that I speak to you I do not speak on My own *authority;* but the Father who dwells in Me does the works. (John 14:10)

> Believe Me that I *am* in the Father and the Father in Me, or else believe Me for the sake of the works themselves. (John 14:11)

> At that day you will know that I *am* in My Father, and you in Me, and I in you. (John 14:20)

> Jesus answered and said to him, "If anyone loves Me, he will keep My word; and My Father will love him, and We will come to him and make Our home with him. (John 14:23)

Please read those verses again and meditate on them until you get a revelation in your spirit of what Jesus is saying. The Father, the Son, and us are all one in essence, but if we are to know the Father, the only way is through Jesus. All other knowledge that we have received of the Father is either incomplete or has been twisted by the enemy and the religious spirit.

Jesus Represents the Tree of Life

What Jesus did not do to an individual while He was on the earth, God won't do to us now. Jesus did not threaten anyone with hell or give anyone sickness to teach them a lesson or make them more holy. And that is not how God the Father operates.

Jesus is the true manifestation of God and the fullness of His character. He was always good; the only thing He couldn't stand was the religious spirit at work in people.

> Beware lest anyone cheat you through philosophy and empty deceit, according to the tradition of men, according to the basic principles of the world, and not according to Christ. For in Him dwells all the fullness of the Godhead bodily; and you are complete in Him, who is the head of all principality and power. (Colossians 2:8-10)

These verses are talking about the Tree of the Knowledge of Good and Evil and the Tree of Life. What is the basis of all philosophies? What is the foundation of the traditions of men? What are the basic principles of the world system? They are all based on good vs. evil, and they all say that if you do good, you will go to heaven, but if you do evil, you will go to hell—or go through the many cycles of life. This is based on which religion you believe.

The verses say that all the philosophies, traditions of men, and basic principles of this world are not according to Christ; they did not originate from Him. Christ represents the Tree of Life. He represents the Father. In Him dwells all the fullness of God in bodily form; and we are complete in Him.

Any other picture that comes to your mind about the Father, other than Christ, is not a true picture. Any imagination that you have of yourself, other than thinking you are complete or perfect in Him, is not coming from the Father or Christ. These come from another kingdom, and we need to reject it.

Any picture that comes to you, other than feeling loved by the Father unconditionally, is not coming from the true God. Why is it that most people don't feel loved by the Father? It's the wrong knowledge they have received about Him. Or because of the wounds and hurts they received from a father figure or their own earthly father.

When we read the Gospels, we should receive true knowledge about two things: the heart of our Father, and His kingdom for which He created us and put us here on the earth. If we do not receive these two things, we cannot understand the true message of the Gospels. That is why the gospel is simply called "good news."

> I have manifested Your name to the men whom You have given Me out of the world. They were Yours, You gave them to Me, and they have kept Your word. (John 17:6)

> O righteous Father! The world has not known You, but I have known You; and these have known that You sent Me. And I have declared to them Your name, and will declare *it*, that the love with which You loved Me may be in them. (John 17:25-26)

This is Jesus's own testimony. He said to the Father that the world has not known Him. If the world had known the true Father, they would believe in Him because He is immensely good and kind. Jesus has known Him and has declared Him to us.

When Peter denied Jesus, it changed the perception of Peter about Jesus, just like it happened for Adam in the beginning. He thought he wouldn't be forgiven, and Jesus wouldn't accept him back as an apostle.

Again, the question Jesus asked him was not 'Why did you do this?' but 'Do you love Me?'

The difference between Adam and Peter is that Adam did not admit his fault and repent, but Peter repented and returned to Jesus. God did not come to the garden to punish Adam; He came to restore him. Likewise, Jesus came to restore Peter, not to punish him.

Jesus is the representation of the Tree of Life; He is the Source of life. Through Jesus, the Tree of Life has been restored to us. When we are returned to the Tree of Life, we will have the right understanding of who God is and His heart toward us. Our broken hearts will be healed by His love and acceptance.

The Trees Compared

Once we are healed and restored, we can then start focusing on our community, city, and then the nations. That is what we read in the book of Revelation. The Tree of Life, its fruit and leaves, will be used for the healing of the nations. I will explain more about this later.

Just like we need healing, nations are also in need of healing because nations are made up of people. If the people are sick and brokenhearted, then the nations also will be sick and brokenhearted. The medicine for healing and restoring nations is people returning to the Tree of Life. This is a revolutionary statement and the solution for earth's problems.

As long as we stay under the Tree of the Knowledge of Good and Evil, we will only see death, destruction, doom, and gloom. We will keep reaping the same results. We can't blame God for it. It is our choice now, under which tree we want to stay. There is no hope with that tree. We will always see only what is wrong and what we can achieve by our own strength. When we transition to the Tree of Life, we will begin to see life, hope, and a bright future. We will see nations coming to the kingdom of God.

All evil, destruction, distortion, and defects that we see in our lives and in the world today, came from eating the fruit of the wrong tree. If that is true, then, to heal, restore, and rebuild everything that is damaged, the solution is to eat again from the right tree—the Tree of Life.

The Tree of Life restores the true nature and character of God in people. They will see God for who He really is for the first time. They will not look at Him through the lens of the knowledge of good and evil.

The Tree of the Knowledge of Good and Evil distorted our knowledge of God. We focused on God dealing with us based on our good behavior and performance, but any belief we have of God, other than *He is love*, comes from this wrong tree.

The Tree of Life gives us the truth: God loves us and blesses us based on *His* goodness and *His* righteousness. That is why Jesus told us to seek His righteousness first.

The Tree of the Knowledge of Good and Evil tells us we are blessed based on our good deeds, behavior, and self-righteousness. As soon as we do something wrong, we will be punished or rejected. Remember, Jesus did not come to punish Peter when he rejected Him, just like the Father did not come to punish Adam—He came to restore him.

With the Tree of Life, the life that is in God becomes our life. Whatever is in God becomes ours by faith.

When we eat from the Tree of Life, we will walk by faith, but the system of good and evil causes us to walk by what we see and how we feel.

With the Tree of Life, God's holiness and righteousness become ours, but when we follow the system of good and evil, we will feel holy only to the extent that we clean ourselves.

With the Tree of Life, God is our Father, and we are His sons and daughters, but with the system of good and evil, God is our Creator and Master, and we are just servants.

Living according to the Tree of the Knowledge of Good and Evil is a life based on our flesh, while the Tree of Life represents a life that is led by the Spirit. This fight will go on our entire life.

I pray that we all will compare and contrast the knowledge of the Father we have in our heart against the knowledge of the Father Jesus came to reveal, and how Jesus lived and dealt with humans. That is the true knowledge and heart of the Father. If we see and understand Jesus, we will see and understand the Father because the Father and Jesus are One and the same. As Jesus said, he who has seen Him has seen the Father.

Deliverance from the Curse

The truth is that once we are saved through Jesus, each of us has to make the choice of which tree we want to be associated with. This is more than a fleeting decision, but a commitment to live a transformed life, regardless of the cost. The tree we eat of will determine the fruit that manifests in our lives. If we remain with the Tree of the Knowledge of Good and Evil, we will be blessed and feel accepted when we do something good, but the moment we fail or make a mistake, we will feel afraid, rejected, guilty, and condemned by God.

When people experience some form of trauma, like sickness, an accident, or any other physical or emotional attack against them, or even sin, a curse will manifest in their lives. They're inclination may be to feel or think it is God who is doing that to them. The truth is that it is not God who is doing any of those things. It is the system doing its work. It is a default setting.

Each individual needs to make the transition from the Tree of the Knowledge of Good and Evil to the Tree of Life. We need to be delivered from the knowledge of good and evil because our whole being and mindset has been programed by that tree. The poison of that fruit has killed billions of people.

We must renounce the Tree of the Knowledge of Good and Evil, its consequences, its fruits, diseases, sicknesses, curses, separation, misconceptions, and the misunderstanding that came to us about our Father. Every defect and belief system that came into us from that tree must go, and we need to accept and activate the Tree of Life and its fruit in us.

Then we need to stay connected to the Tree of Life. Unknowingly, ninety percent of what we do in church and our belief system has been formed and defined by the wrong tree and its fruit. It is time to make the transition.

We must attach ourselves to the Tree of Life by faith. We will be tempted to go back to the wrong tree again, but we need to intentionally choose to stay with the right tree. Only there will we find life and life more abundantly.

Jesus is the manifestation of the Tree of Life. The Bible says, "In Him was life, and the life was the light of men" (John 1:4). The life that we see in Jesus is the true light for all people. Jesus did not bless, accept, or heal people based on their good works or performance; it was all based on His goodness. The Father did not love Jesus based on His performance or ministry. Jesus said the Father loves us with the same love He loved Jesus.

> As the Father loved Me, I also have loved you; abide in My love. (John 15:9)

> I in them, and You in Me; that they may be made perfect in one, and that the world may know that You have sent Me, and have loved them as You have loved Me. (John 17:23)

> Father, I desire that they also whom You gave Me may be with Me where I am, that they may behold My glory which You have given Me; for You loved Me before the foundation of the world. (John 17:24)

> And I have declared to them Your name, and will declare *it,* that the love with which You loved Me may be in them, and I in them. (John 17:26)

The above verses say that the Father loved Jesus before the foundation of the world, and He loves each one of us with the same love. God did not start loving us after we were saved. Jesus wants us to experience the same love that the Father has loved Him with—unconditional love.

To understand clearly what I am writing here, it will be helpful if the reader has the background knowledge of some of the books this ministry has previously published, especially *Rediscovering the Lost Kingdom* and *God's Original Design*. These two books contain the foundational information and revelation on which this and other books have been built.

You may wonder if this type of doctrine will cause people to live in sin. Do you want to know the ultimate key to overcoming sin? The first commandment is the key to overcoming sin. It is to love the Lord our God with all our heart, with all our soul, with all our mind, and with all our strength. Then, to love our neighbor as we love ourselves. When you truly love someone, you won't do anything to hurt that person. If we do something by mistake, we will be quick to apologize and to ask for their forgiveness.

When we love God with all of our heart, soul, mind, and strength, we won't have any tendency to sin. When we abide in His love, sin won't have any hold on us. When we are under the Tree of Life, death loses its grip. Many try to obey all the commandments or observe some rules and regulations, or rituals, thinking that is how to love the Lord. No, He wants us to love Him with all our heart, not all our rules, and not by keeping some holidays or wearing some kind of jewelry.

When we love our neighbors, we won't sin against them either. If I truly love my neighbor or my friend, then I won't lie to him, and I won't steal, covet, or murder. Love is the fulfillment of the law (Romans 13:9-10).

Healing of the Nations

> And he showed me a pure river of water of life, clear as crystal, procceding from the throne of God and of the Lamb. In the middle of its street, and on either side of the river, *was* the tree of life, which bore twelve fruits, each *tree* yielding its fruit every month. The leaves of the tree *were* for the healing of the nations. (Revelation 22:1-2)

All of creation came under the bondage of corruption because of the fall of Adam, so God planned to redeem the whole creation. Redemption is part of our salvation. If people are cursed and bound, then whatever they do will be cursed and bound. We spread and multiply what we carry and have wherever we go. If we carry hope and healing, we will spread hope and healing wherever we go. If we carry doom, gloom, and despair, we will spread that wherever we go.

God wants to heal nations. The "medicine" to heal the nations is the Tree of Life. Once we are restored to our Father as sons and daughters and understand His heart and dream for the earth and nations, we will start partnering with Him to fulfill His dream.

As we saw in the above verses, the Tree of Life and the river of life are restored back to us. When people read the book of Revelation, they think about it futuristically, just like most believers think about the kingdom. Again, God and His Word are timeless. This means that we can tap into what is written in God's Word, by faith at any time.

People like Abraham and David tapped into what God would offer through Christ way before He died on the cross. How? Because, by faith, they understood and tapped into the timeless revelation that the Lamb was slain before the foundation of the world. That's how we should be operating as God's children—living by faith.

We read in the above verse that the tree produced twelve fruits for each month of the year. And the leaves of the tree *were* for the healing of the nations. This is written in past tense, not in future tense. I believe the twelve fruits are the twelve components of the kingdom.

The kingdom of God is the solution for every problem the earth has. Each component of the kingdom is the solution to the problems the nations of the earth are currently facing. For healing of the economy of our nation, the solution, or the medicine, is Kingdom Economy.

The solution, or medicine, for the healing of marriages and families is Kingdom Family. The education system of this world is broken and sick, so the solution is Kingdom Education. For every problem we have in our lives and in our nations, there is a solution in God's kingdom. But it says the leaves of the tree were for the healing of the nations. Leaves represent each kingdom citizen who will carry this healing to the nations, because each individual is called by God to manifest an aspect of His kingdom.

Each of us carries a "piece" of the kingdom of God in our spirit man. We are the leaves of the Tree of Life. When each one of us manifests the kingdom of God based on our calling, this healing process of nations will begin.

Each one of us is called to manifest at least one of the components of the kingdom of God. That is what I am going to discuss in the next chapter.

Once we understand the true nature of God, then we are ready to be ruled by Him. The government of God will manifest among us. That is the next chapter. The only government we have known so far is based on the Tree of the Knowledge of Good and Evil. The old covenant was also based on this same tree. Every constitution we see out there was derived from the law of Moses. Jesus said:

> The law and the prophets *were* until John. Since that time the kingdom of God has been preached, and everyone is pressing into it. (Luke 16:16)

This means the Tree of the Knowledge of Good and Evil (the law) was only until John. Since that time, the kingdom of God, which operates under the Tree of Life, sonship, and God's righteousness, has been preached, and everyone is pressing into it.

We haven't yet had an opportunity to be governed by the Tree of Life. The true government of God will only work when we are under the Tree of Life. Everything else will bring us back into bondage. We are ready to be governed by God when we are able to love Him with all our heart, soul, mind, and strength. Love is the foundation of His kingdom.

The New Heaven and the New Earth

The Tree of the Knowledge of Good and Evil not only created the wrong perception of the Father in us, but it distorted how we see ourselves. After the fall, Adam couldn't see anything good in him. He only saw his flaws and what was wrong with him. He told God He doesn't want to come near to Him because he felt fearful, naked, and rejected. He hid himself from God. That is what most people on this earth do today. They don't believe God will accept them, so they hide or ran away from Him.

This tree distorted our vision because it opened the wrong set of eyes in us, which causes us to see only the flaws in others and in the world around us. That is how the doom, gloom, and despair theology came into the church. They have been waiting for the end of this world and the destruction of the earth for the last two thousand years. Because they can't see anything good, they don't believe it can be repaired or restored.

When we transition to the Tree of Life, our perception of God will be repaired, and then we will begin to see good in ourselves—the new man that was created in Christ Jesus. Once we see the new man, and the world and the earth through the eyes of that new man, we will begin to see the good in everything. Instead of speaking death, we will begin to speak life. Not only that, but wherever we go, we will bring that same life. This is the river of life from Revelation 22:1-2.

> A healing tongue is a tree of life, but a deceitful one crushes the spirit. (Proverbs 15:4, TLV)

We have been cursing and speaking death and destruction over this earth and everything in it for a long time. It is time to speak life and restoration. Jesus said that out of our belly shall flow rivers of living water (John 7:38). It is the words of life that Jesus was talking about. Wherever that river flows, it will cause life to spring forth. Whatever is dead when this river touches it, will come back to life. We are that river, and we carry that river of life inside of us. When we look at the world and the earth through the eyes of the Tree of Life and the river of life, all of a sudden, we will begin to see hope, new life, and restoration. Ezekiel prophesied about this river.

> And it shall be *that* every living thing that moves, wherever the rivers go, will live. There will be a very great multitude of fish, because these waters go there; for they will be healed, and everything will live wherever the river goes. (Ezekiel 47:9)

When mankind is restored back to the Tree of Life and its fruit, as God originally intended, the nations will be healed and restored back to God as well. This is how the whole earth is going to be restored and healed and become how it was in Genesis chapters 1 & 2.

In Revelation 21:1-4, we read about a new heaven and a new earth.

> Now I saw a new heaven and a new earth, for the first heaven and the first earth had passed away. Also there was no more sea. Then I, John, saw the holy city, New Jerusalem, coming down out of heaven from God, prepared as a bride adorned for her husband. And I heard a loud voice from heaven saying, "Behold, the tabernacle of God *is* with men, and He will dwell with them, and they shall be His people. God Himself will be with them *and be* their God. And God will wipe away every tear from their eyes; there shall be no more death, nor sorrow, nor crying. There shall be no more pain, for the former things have passed away."

Whatever comes under the dominion of Christ is considered a new creation. According to 2 Corinthians 5:17, when we are in Christ, we are considered a new creation. Old things are passed away and everything becomes new.

Do you see the similarities between the verses in Revelation 21 and the one above? When any part of this earth comes under the dominion of Christ, that part is declared new. When the whole earth and heaven come under the rulership or dominion of Christ, they will be called a new heaven and a new earth.

The earth, nations, and the people are in the process of being healed and restored. That is why, though we read about a new heaven and a new earth in Revelation 21, we read in Revelation 22:2 about the healing of nations. Healing is a process.

> Whom heaven must receive until the times of restoration of all things, which God has spoken by the mouth of all His holy prophets since the world began. (Acts 3:21)

Chapter 8

The Government of God - Part 1

However, they will become subjects to him so that they may learn the difference between serving Me and serving the kings of the earth. (2 Chronicles 12:8 TLV)

A book about a kingdom nation would be incomplete without writing about the government of God. Every nation is required to have a government. Without a government, a nation cannot function.

When we say that God is reigning over us, what type of government are we talking about? Democratic, where we elect a righteous or Christian leader every few years to be on the top of the food chain? Socialistic, where the government owns and controls all enterprise? Or a monarchy, where one man or woman rules over the territory and people? Is it capitalistic, where only the smart ones outsmart everyone else and get the best and the most of everything? No.

Understanding Kingdom Government

In the Old Testament, when the people asked for a leader or a king to rule over them like other nations, it very much displeased God. He said they rejected Him from reigning over them. How did God plan to reign over them without a king or a leader? What kind of governing system did He have in His mind?

> Then all the elders of Israel gathered together and came to Samuel at Ramah, and said to him, "Look, you are old, and your sons do not walk in your ways. Now make us a king to judge us like all the nations." But the thing displeased Samuel when they said, "Give us a king to judge us." So Sam- uel prayed to the LORD. And the LORD said to Samuel, "Heed the voice of the people in all that they say to you; for they have not rejected you, but they have rejected Me, that I should not reign over them. (1 Samuel 8:4-7)

When we say that Christ is going to rule the whole earth, how is He going to do it practically? If the capital is going to be in Jerusalem, in the Middle East, how will He manage what happens in a town in Venezuela?

Kingdom Government is based on theocracy. Each individual is governed by his or her Creator by His Spirit within them. That's why He put His Spirit in each one of us, so everyone is connected to Him individually. That is why God said He wants to pour out His Spirit upon all flesh in the last days, so everyone can be led and be taught by Him. That is what happened on the day of Pentecost.

> And it shall come to pass in the last days, says God, That I will pour out of My Spirit on all flesh;
> Your sons and your daughters shall prophesy, Your young men shall see visions,
> Your old men shall dream dreams.
> And on My menservants and on My maidservants I will pour out My Spirit in those days;
> And they shall prophesy. (Acts 2:17-18)

Please notice that when God pours out His Spirit upon all flesh, three things must happen; they will prophesy, see visions, and see dreams. All three results are spiritual in nature, which means they originated first in the invisible realm. People have to hear or see what is in the Spirit before they can prophesy. Visions and dreams have to do with capturing what is in heaven—what God wants to manifest on the earth—and then releasing it. That is the purpose behind God pouring out His Spirit; to be governed by Him and to manifest heaven on earth.

The Holy Spirit holds the blueprints of God. He searches out the deep things of God and knows the mind of God.

He is the link between us and God the Father (1 Corinthians 2:10-12).

> Then I will give them one heart, and I will put a new spirit within them, and take the stony heart out of their flesh, and give them a heart of flesh, that they may walk in My statutes and keep My judgments and do them; and they shall be My people, and I will be their God. (Ezekiel 11:19-20)

> For this *is* the covenant that I will make with the house of Israel after those days, says the LORD: I will put My laws in their mind and write them on their hearts; and I will be their God, and they shall be My people. (Hebrews 8:10)

> This *is* the covenant that I will make with them after those days, says the LORD: I will put My laws into their hearts, and in their minds I will write them. (Hebrews 10:16)

When Kingdom Government manifests, it will function the following way:

None of them shall teach his neighbor, and none his brother, saying, "Know the Lord," for all shall know Me, from the least of them to the greatest of them. For I will be merciful to their unrighteousness, and their sins and their lawless deeds I will remember no more. (Hebrews 8:11-12)

That doesn't mean it's a loose system with everyone just doing whatever they want. There has to be accountability on all fronts. That's why God doesn't want one person on top of the ladder. It shouldn't be a ladder or a pyramid system, but a circle, where we all stand on the same level and ground, seeing each other face to face, and connected to each other. We honor and hold each other in love and unity. And we maximize the opportunities and resources God has given to us, not for personal gratification or gain, but to honor our King and establish His kingdom and will on earth as one family in Christ.

God never wanted to give us laws or rules and regulations. Those also came because of sin and the fall. The law was the by-product of Adam activating a system of life based on the knowledge of good and evil.

The majority of the church world is still under the old covenant. They try to put the Ten Commandments in public squares and in government buildings, and though they have good intentions, the spirit that works behind this is not the Holy Spirit, but the spirit that works in the gentile leaders.

God did not give authority to anyone to rule over people or to dominate them. We may have done it out of ignorance or immaturity, but since we now know the truth, let's go back to the kingdom style of government and management.

The Holy Spirit has been sent to reveal to us the things that have been given freely to us by our Father God (1 Corinthians 2:12). Instead of knowing, receiving, and managing what has been given to us by our

Father, we went after the gifts of the Holy Spirit because we thought that verse is talking about gifts.

The gifts of the Holy Spirit are given to us to bring people into the kingdom. They are "tools" to accomplish a task for the King in the kingdom, not a means to build a ministry or to make money for survival. Because of insecurity and a lack of understanding, people all over the world went after the gifts to make themselves feel significant and secure. The gifts of the Holy Spirit have been used for personal gain. Jesus gave a stern warning to these people in Matthew 7:21-22.

The Government of David

We won't understand the kingdom of God and the government of God without understanding the life of David.

It was through David whom God chose to establish His kingdom and government in Israel.

Without David, there is no kingdom of God on earth. He plays such an important role in the over-all purpose of God concerning the earth, not because he was a holy or perfect man, but because of his revelation about the kingdom of God.

David was the first human being to receive the revelation of the kingdom of God, and he began to write about it in the Psalms. When God looked upon the earth, He found one man who understood who God is, His purpose, and about His kingdom. God was very happy to find this man. He spoke of him and said that he is a man after His heart.

When God finds a man or a woman like that, He will go to any length to protect, preserve, and provide for them. They will receive kingdom diplomatic immunity. In human terms, I can say they become His favorites. That is why the Bible says wherever David went, God

THE BIRTHING OF A KINGDOM NATION

preserved him and gave him victory. The good news is that you can become His favorite if you receive the revelation of His kingdom.

David is the man who never lost a battle. In every battle he fought, God gave him victory. He had many personal and family issues and challenges, but he learned to humble himself before God and navigate all of life's storms.

Every human carries a "piece" of kingdom government within them. God put that in there to help them govern themselves. That is why Jesus said the kingdom of God is within you (Luke 17:21). In other words, He is saying the government of God is within you. We cannot separate God's kingdom from His government; they are inseparable. Paul also said that the laws of God are written within the human conscious (Romans 2:14-15). Even though they do not know God, they have no excuse.

When people are not aware of the government of God within them, we need rules and regulations to manage people. We have "law enforcement" in every country that we call the police force. They are there to enforce the constitutional laws of that government and people. God's plan for mankind is to govern from within: the laws written in their hearts and conscious by Him.

The solution to every crime and all violence and evil that we see on the earth today is not to legislate more righteous or Christian laws and then force people to obey them, but to bring people into awareness of who they are and what is in them. That is why we need to preach the gospel of the kingdom—not to just take them to heaven but to bring the revelation of what is in them and who they are.

I wondered many times why God did not ask anyone to take over heathen kings or kingdoms. Joseph, Moses, or Daniel did not do that. We don't see that in Bible. Later, I understood that it's because that's not the type of government He has in mind. They were the kingdoms of this world or the governments of the gentiles. Kingdom Government and the world's government operate on entirely different systems.

It is sad to see Christians trying to take over the governments of this world for the sake of establishing a more "righteous or Christian government." They are in error because they think Kingdom Government is when a Christian or "good person" rules over everyone else.

That's the gentile form of government. God never wanted such leaders or government systems. They asked for it, and that's why He allowed it.

That is why Jesus said to come to Him and to learn from Him (Matthew 11:29). What do we need to learn from Him? If we need to know what life is, we need to learn from Jesus. Why? Because He is Life. If we need to know what truth is, we need to learn from Jesus. Why? Because He is the Truth. If we need to know peace, real and everlasting peace, we need to receive it from Him because He is the Prince of Peace.

If we need to know how to relate with our heavenly Father, and how to live as a son, we need to learn from Jesus how He related with His heavenly Father. Jesus is our model, or the prototype of the human species. In Him was life, and the life is the light of men (John 1:4). He is the Way to the Father. This means that Jesus came to reveal the Father and His heart toward humanity. Now people can clear the misunderstanding they had in their hearts about the Father.

Without David, there is no kingdom of God on the earth. He is the only man who established God's kingdom and His government in a practical sense that we know of.

When we study what David did to establish God's kingdom and government, we will receive a clear understanding of how we are to function as a kingdom nation now.

There are four things that both Testaments talk about concerning David. Those four components are uniquely important to the kingdom and government of God on the earth. We will discuss them in detail, according to the grace He has given me.

Led By the Spirit

Both the Old and New Testaments talk about an important quality a child of God is required to possess to live a kingdom life. That is the ability to be led by the Spirit of God. In that one quality hangs everything else we do, and whether we will be successful or not. One of the greatest tragedies in life is to be successful in the wrong thing, meaning successful in something that you were not called to do, as Jesus warned us in Matthew 7:22-23.

How can a nation function without a person on the top or without a head of state? Jesus needs to be the Person on top: the head of every person, state, and nation. From Him flows the issues of life and all authority He carries—He is the King and the government.

We read about elders in both the Old and New Testament. Elders are like managers. Their job is to make sure everything is running the way it is supposed to run. They are not above the people; they are among us and from us, like the twenty-four elders in heaven that we read about in the book of Revelation. God uses the same system in heaven. We need to follow the same pattern. Our job is to see what's happening in heaven and copy it on the earth.

> Around the throne *were* twenty-four thrones, and on the thrones I saw twenty-four elders sitting, clothed in white robes; and they had crowns of gold on their heads. (Revelation 4:4)

THE GOVERNMENT OF GOD - PART 1

Notice the formation and the seating arrangement of the thrones in heaven. They are arranged in a circle, rather than a pyramid or ladder. The current leadership styles and structures we follow in churches really need to take a look at this. Most of them are following the gentile or the Babylonian system.

That's why we see that Paul appointed elders in every city in which he started an Ekklesia (Acts 14:23; 20:17; Titus 1:5). It was the elders who ran the day-to-day affairs of an Ekklesia, not the pastors. In the kingdom nation, we need to have elders in every city and town who are in charge of the different components of the kingdom. Their job is to make sure the Ekklesia in that town is functioning as it should and see that God's will is being accomplished in that region.

Each city should have twelve elders in charge of administering the kingdom of God in that region. This is the pattern the early church followed. It is the pattern that was established in heaven.

How did God plan to rule this earth through humans? What kind of government was it? We receive a glimpse of this in Genesis chapters 1 & 2, and in the nation of Israel.

God would meet with Adam and Eve in the cool of the day. What did they discuss? What were the topics of their discussion? Adam and Eve were not singing for half an hour to God to make Him happy. It was an official governmental meeting. It was a family meeting.

It was a partnership between God and man. Remember that it has always been God's plan to dwell in humans to accomplish His will and plan on earth through them.

He wanted each individual to be governed by Him through His Spirit. Not by laws written in a paper, a scroll, or on a rock, but by His laws written in the hearts of humans. Not ruled by any external force, rules and regulations, fear of punishment, or influence of others, but from within—from our spirit man, who is yielded to God and His Spirit. It is called self-control or the temperance of human will. In the kingdom of God, it is called self-government.

God wants us to obey Him, not because of fear, but because we love Him. Only when we understand His love for us will we be able to do what He wants us to do. Until then, everything is pretense and fake. That's the first and foremost commandment (Mark 12:29-31). Many people try to obey God because of the fear of man or the fear of punishment; but, in secret, they live in all kinds of sin.

Why was God grieved when the people of Israel asked Samuel to give them a king like other nations? God never wanted a government like that. He does not want His people to be ruled by any other external force or by pressure or fear.

God doesn't want people to lord over or dominate others. Jesus said that's the gentile way of ruling. They wanted a king and a government like the gentile nations.

Everything Jesus taught and preached was to present the contrast between how His kingdom and its components work compared to the kings and kingdoms of this world and their components. His kingdom is not of this world.

Old and New Covenants

Moses wrote of the blessing of the LORD, "If you *hear the voice of the Lord* and indeed obey His commandments" (Deuteronomy 30:9-10). God wanted them to hear His voice and obey Him (Psalm 95:7-8). It's the same in the New Covenant; Jesus said, "My sheep hear my voice." (John 10:16 & 27)

Old covenant laws were written on tablets of stone, but God wants His laws to be written in our hearts. That's why He says no one will be taught by the people, saying, "know the Lord," everyone will know Him and walk with Him. (Hebrews 8:11-12)

In the old covenant, God would choose one person to hear His voice, and then that person went and shared with the people what He wanted to tell them. They had to obey what they heard. If they disobeyed, it was as if they were disobeying God.

It was usually a priest or a prophet who spoke to the people the word of the Lord. Priests taught the written Word of God, or the laws (logos), and the prophets brought the "now" word from the Lord, the rhema. Prophets heard and told the people what they must do at any given time. Priests laid the foundation and taught them His statues, precepts, and commandments.

There is a huge difference between hearing and following the *voice of God* and reading and following the statues and precepts of God that are written on a paper or on a tablet. One requires active hearing with our spirit man, and the other only requires our mind.

When everyone is led by the Holy Spirit and lives by hearing the voice of God, there won't be any contradictions or schisms because they are all led by the same Spirit. They won't commit any sins because they will love each other as they should. When someone is led by a spirit other than the Spirit of God, division or strife comes.

The Spirit of God is not a spirit of confusion. When two people are led by the Spirit of God, they will agree and reach the same conclusion. Will people ever do wrong in Kingdom Government? Yes, of course, on this earth, we all miss God every now and then. But we are in the process of becoming like Jesus. The sooner we learn from our mistakes and not repeat them, all will be well.

That is what happened in the early church. When the apostles came together to decide regarding the gentile believers, whether or not they should keep the laws of Moses, in the beginning, there was a great dispute among them. But at the end, they came to the same conclusion because they decided to yield to the Holy Spirit. They said, "For it seemed good to the Holy Spirit, and to us." (Acts 15:28)

Whenever one man or woman rules over others, we miss God, and we slip into the gentile style of leadership. That's why the Bible doesn't teach on the subject of leadership. In leadership, there is always one man or woman at the top of the ladder.

In the kingdom of God, all sons and daughters sit with the King around the table. It's a family business meeting.

Each one will have a different role and responsibility, but no one is above another.

In the new covenant, everyone has the opportunity to hear the voice of God and be led by His Spirit. The reason there is so much division in the body of Christ is because everyone is not led by the same spirit. We don't follow the kingdom style of governance but the gentile leadership style. To be honest, it is sad to say that many don't even believe in the same Jesus that is mentioned in the Bible.

There are many spirits and Jesuses on the earth today (2 Corinthians 11:4). They are not from God. They are demon spirits pretending to be an angel of light (2 Corinthians 11:14). How do we differentiate them? We know them by their fruits. They won't be building God's kingdom but their own little kingdoms and lording over people— appointing themselves as leaders and as kings and queens.

Their god is their belly (Philippians 3:19). They are looking for positions and titles. They want the prominent seats and recognition. They want to make a name for themselves.

The True Purpose for the Fivefold Ministry

Fivefold ministry was given to the church to equip the saints to hear the voice of God, to be led by the Holy Spirit, and to establish them in the kingdom of their Father as sons and daughters— to help them find their place in their Father's house and function in it.

Instead of this, todays "fivefold ministers" try to control people. They place themselves in the place of God and expect people to follow their leadership and their teachings. They are not training people to follow God.

How do we distinguish a true fivefold minister from a gentile leader who is pretending to be a fivefold minister? If they are not equipping and releasing the people to become what God created them to be, they are gentile leaders. They are not building God's kingdom, but an enterprise.

If they are not training the people to find their position as sons and their place in their Fathers kingdom, and if they are not raising up the sons and daughters of God, they are not true ministers. They are there for their own personal gain.

If they are not building God's kingdom on earth, they are not true servants of God. Many servants of God have been deceived because they just didn't know the truth. They followed what they knew and what they were taught by the religious spirit.

That's why we have these resources available to anyone who wants them. They can read and study these books on the kingdom of God. They can also join the Kingdom University and discover their God-given purpose and calling.

How Kingdom Government Should Work

If you want to know how the government of God works, look at Jesus and how He dealt with the people around Him. He was not forcing anyone to believe in Him. He was not walking around with a cape on His back with "Savior of the world" written on it. There was no display board with the Ten Commandments written on the front of it. Neither was He going from town to town conducting musicals or concerts.

In the Gospels, we see how Jesus governed the people—with righteousness, truth, and mercy. Mercy triumphed over judgment.

Jesus was not a "law enforcement" officer. That is what Christians try to do today. They want to elect a "Christian" president or governor and enforce people to obey the truth or righteous laws. It won't work. Pretty soon, those rulers will become tyrants or dictators. Those are gentile leaders with a gentile style of leadership.

That's not how Kingdom Government works. God's kingdom is governed by love because God is love. Righteousness and justice are the foundation of His throne (Psalm 97:2). We must teach and train people to be led by the Spirit and obey God from within.

Kingdom Government is when a person is governed by his own born-again spirit, being led by the Holy Spirit, and doing what is right by obeying the laws of God written on his or her heart and conscious. They are led from within. When this happens, every form of evil will end. Crime will diminish, and violence in our streets will stop.

We are commanded to love God and love our neighbors as we love ourselves. When we love our neighbor, we won't do any evil to them. We won't steal from them; we won't covet anything they have. We won't kill or do any harm to others. That's why the Bible says love is the fulfillment of the law (Romans 13:9-10).

We will have elders, instructors, teachers, facilitators, and overseers to manage, train, and equip in every aspect of the kingdom, in every region. Their job is to instruct us and train us in the ways of God. They are not there to control or rule over people but to facilitate God's rule and reign. Ultimately, we are supposed to be governed by God by being led by His Spirit. Those who are led by the Spirit of God are the sons of God (Romans 8:14).

The Process of Governing

There are four very important components of God's Kingdom Government on earth. Without a clear understanding about these components, we won't be able to establish God's kingdom on earth the way He wants it.

Do you remember what happened in the Old Testament? They rejected God from ruling over them and chose the way of the gentiles. There are different empires and organizations that claim they represent God's kingdom on earth, but they are not authentic.

David was the first human to understand how the government of God works in relation to the earth and humans. I believe he was led by the Holy Spirit in what he was doing when it came to fulfilling what God wanted him to do. He was a man after God's own heart, meaning, he understood who God is and what He wants to see accomplished on the earth. That is why God said he was one "who will do all My will."

> And when He had removed him, He raised up for them David as king, to whom also He gave testimony and said, "I have found David the *son* of Jesse, a man after My *own* heart, who will do all My will." (Acts 13:22)

When it comes to the government of God, there are four things the Bible mentions in relation to David: the Son of David, the tabernacle of David, the throne of David, and the key of David. Only when we understand what they all mean, their purpose and the function of each of them, can we partner with God in establishing His kingdom and will on earth. Each of these components plays an integral role in the function of God's government. One won't work without the other. They have to work together in unison. Let's explore each of them and what they mean.

Chapter 9

The Government of God - Part 2

The book of the genealogy of Jesus Christ, the Son of David, the Son of Abraham. (Matthew 1:1)

To understand the government of Christ on the earth, we need to understand four important components revealed through the life of David. In the following pages, we are going to explore them one by one.

The Son of David

*"What do you think about the Christ? Whose Son is He?" They said to Him, "*The Son* of David." (Matthew 22:42)*

David is the first human being who received the revelation of who God is, His purpose for the earth and mankind, and His kingdom. When God looked from heaven, He saw one human being on the face of all the earth who understood who He is and what He wanted done on the earth.

Because of the revelation David received of God's kingdom, God made an unconditional covenant with David and his descendants. God sent the prophet Nathan to speak the following words to David. Please don't skip reading these verses:

> Now therefore, thus shall you say to My servant David, 'Thus says the LORD of hosts: "I took you from the sheepfold, from following the sheep, to be ruler over My people, over Israel. And I have been with you wherever you have gone, and have cut off all your enemies from before you, and have made you a great name, like the name of the great men who *are* on the earth. Moreover I will appoint a place for My people Israel, and will plant them, that they may dwell in a place of their own and move no more; nor shall the sons of wickedness oppress them anymore, as previously, since the time that I commanded judges *to be* over My people Israel, and have caused you to rest from all your enemies." Also the LORD tells you that He will make you a house.
>
> "When your days are fulfilled and you rest with your fathers, I will set up your seed after you, who will come from your body, and I will establish his kingdom. He shall build a house for My name, and I will establish the throne of his kingdom forever. I will be his Father, and he shall be My son.
>
> If he commits iniquity, I will chasten him with the rod of men and with the blows of the sons of men. But My mercy shall not depart from him, as I took *it* from Saul, whom I removed from before you. And your house and your kingdom shall be established forever before you. Your throne shall be established forever."' (2 Samuel 7:8-16)

The last part of that prophetic covenant is very important in order to understand the course of history and the purpose of God for planet earth, and the process He put in place in fulfilling it. The most important part of God's government is the King Himself, the Son of

David, who is the King of this kingdom nation. Without Him, there is no kingdom. This King is Jesus Christ, the Son of the living God.

God promised David that his seed would sit on his throne, and that He will establish His kingdom forever. His house and his kingdom shall be established forever, and the throne shall be established forever.

The immediate seed God is talking about in the above verse is Solomon, who was next in line to take over David's throne. But there is a spiritual and eternal implication to that word "seed." It is a singular word.

That Seed is Jesus Christ, who would come from David's lineage to inherit his throne and rule this earth and the house of Jacob forever and ever. At the birth of Jesus Christ, this prophecy was fulfilled. We read about it in the following verses. An angel appeared to Mary and told her the following:

> And behold, you will conceive in your womb and bring forth a Son, and shall call His name JESUS. He will be great, and will be called the Son of the Highest; and the Lord God will give Him the throne of His father David. And He will reign over the house of Jacob forever, and of His kingdom there will be no end. (Luke 1:31-33)

The angel Gabriel was talking about the birth of Jesus Christ. That is how Jesus is called the Son of David. Not very many understood this in Israel at that time. This can be revealed only through the Holy Spirit. The people who recognized Jesus as the Messiah and as the Son of David were the most unlikely people.

We have been waiting for Jesus to come and establish His kingdom and throne in Jerusalem and rule, without knowing that that prophecy was fulfilled by His birth. He is waiting for the Kingdom Nation to be birthed so He can come and rule the earth through us. Below are

THE BIRTHING OF A KINGDOM NATION

other verses that show that by the birth of Jesus Christ the prophecy was fulfilled.

> For unto us a Child is born,
> Unto us a Son is given;
> And the government will be upon His shoulder. And His name will be called
> Wonderful, Counselor, Mighty God, Everlasting Father, Prince of Peace.
> Of the increase of *His* government and peace
> *There will be* no end,
> Upon the throne of David and over His kingdom,
> To order it and establish it with judgment and justice From that time forward, even forever.
> The zeal of the Lord of hosts will perform this. (Isaiah 9:6-7)

The scholars and the wise did not understand it. They failed to recognize their Messiah. But people who were rejected by scholars and the religious circle received this revelation. Peter preached about it on the day of Pentecost. That is how he preached the gospel of the kingdom that day, because his audience were Jewish people that had come to Jerusalem for the feast of Pentecost.

> Men *and* brethren, let *me* speak freely to you of the patriarch David, that he is both dead and buried, and his tomb is with us to this day. Therefore, being a prophet, and knowing that God had sworn with an oath to him that of the fruit of his body, according to the flesh, He would raise up the Christ to sit on his throne. (Acts 2:29-30)

The first person to whom Jesus revealed Himself as the Messiah was the Samaritan woman. One of the other people who understood this revelation was a blind man called Bartimaeus. Even today, the same thing happens. The kingdom of God has been hidden from the wise and prudent, but the simple and the most unlikely people capture it in their spirit.

There was a blind man who lived in Israel during Jesus's time, and was called Bartimaeus (Mark 10:46-52). He was born blind and lived by begging on the street. He had no place or status in society. He was an outcast. People thought he was born blind because of some sin or curse of his parents. He had nothing to look forward to, until one day, when he was begging by the road that went to Jericho. That day was different than any other day he had in his life.

As he sat by the road and begged to the people walking by, he heard the noise and chattering of the crowd passing him by. It was unusual for that day. It was not any special day or a day of feast to have such a crowd passing at once. He became curious and asked one of the pedestrians what it was all about.

Someone replied to him and said that Jesus of Nazareth was passing by. Though Bartimaeus was born blind, he was not an ordinary blind man. He had an inquisitive nature in the spirit. He was not blind in his spirit. He could see and understand things in the spirit that most people, including the well-educated, couldn't see or understand.

When he heard that Jesus of Nazareth was passing by, something exploded in his spirit-man. Know that this fellow never went into the temple. He had never seen nor read a scroll or scripture. He never went to school to study anything, but he was learning much more important things from the school of the Spirit. In the spirit, he was a well educated man. To God, that's what matters the most.

When he heard the name, Jesus of Nazareth, he knew his day and moment had come. It was the day of his deliverance and healing, and he knew that if he missed that moment, he would be lost forever. It was like God the Father orchestrated Jesus and His team to pass by that road just for this man.

Bartimaeus was destined to be a beggar for the rest of his life. He was an outcast and untouchable. Nobody wanted to be his friend, and begging was his mode of survival. But understand this, God is the Friend of those who are humble in heart and lowly in spirit. He is not impressed with our worldly education or eloquence.

In the spirit, Bartimaeus understood this Jesus of Nazareth that was passing him by is the Messiah, the Son of David. He began to cry out calling Jesus the Son of David. He didn't call Him Jesus of Nazareth. Where did this blind man receive the idea or the revelation that Jesus of Nazareth is the Son of David?

He cried out because he couldn't miss that moment. It was the opportunity of a lifetime. That day would change the rest of his life, and rewrite his destiny and the destinies of the generations after him.

People began to tell him to be quiet because he was making too much noise. The more people tried to quiet him, the more he cried out at the top of his lungs. He didn't pay any attention to those people who told him to be quiet; he shouted and cried even louder, "Jesus, Son of David, have mercy on me!"

The Bible says that Jesus stood still. Time stopped for a moment. All of heaven, earth, and the Creator of the universe paid attention to the cry of a blind man. Imagine the desperation this man felt in his spirit. Have you ever been desperate like that for God in your life? So desperate that you couldn't miss a moment, and you knew in your spirit that if you did, it would be the loss of a lifetime. Pay attention to those moments. Don't waste them.

Jesus told the people to bring that blind man to Him. Why? He recognized in the Spirit that someone used the key of David and put a demand on the covenantal blessing that God had made with David regarding his house and his throne hundreds of years before.

Remember the authority the key of David carries in the spirit. If you use it and open something, no one can close it. If you use it to open a time gate in the spirit, no one can close that opportunity.

Why did this blind man call Jesus the Son of David rather than Jesus of Nazareth? (Mark 10:47). They knew the Messiah would come and that He would be the Son of David. Somehow, this blind man received the revelation in his spirit that Jesus of Nazareth is the Messiah, the Son of David.

The religious leaders of that day did not understand it. The well-educated in the temple couldn't comprehend it. They didn't grasp that Jesus is the Son of David, who came to inherit the throne and the key of David, and to rule the house of Jacob forever and ever.

This blind man used the key of David and opened the treasury of God's kingdom. Jesus, who is the descendant of David, the keeper and heir of that treasury and throne, must stop and administer justice to the needy.

> A bruised reed He will not break, and smoking flax He will not quench, Till He sends forth justice to victory. (Matthew 12:20)

Bartimaeus was a bruised reed, a smoking flax that was left to die. His hope was only death. Nothing better was spoken of his future. But he had a very secret and sacred treasure in the spirit. The revelation of the kingdom of God and His Messiah, the Son of David. He could use it to open something, and no one could close it.

The crowd couldn't stop or silence him. They couldn't steal that moment from him. He was unstoppable. He got hold of the key of David. It was all seven dimensions of the key of David working at once. He was praising Jesus by calling Him the Son of David, and that's how he opened the treasury of the kingdom of heaven. He tapped into the revelation of sonship by calling Jesus a Son.

Heaven had to stop for this man. People went and brought him to Jesus. Jesus asked him, "What do you want Me to do for you?" Meaning, which blessing of the house of David do you need? Which blessing from the treasury of the kingdom of God do you need?

He put a demand on the covenantal blessing God had made with the house of David. Everything you need in your life is part of that blessing: your healing, provision, your destiny, protection; anything and everything is included in that covenant.

That's why Jesus told us to seek His kingdom and His righteousness FIRST, and then all the things we need will be added to us. When you seek God's kingdom, you get to access the covenantal blessing of the house of David and his throne in your life.

Just like we became the children of Abraham by faith in Jesus Christ, when we discover God's kingdom, we become an heir of David and the covenant God made with him. We become a part of the ruling class; a part of his throne and the crown.

When you use the key of David by faith, you can access any blessing in the kingdom of God. Your healing is part of this blessing. Your provision is part of this blessing. You become unstoppable for God.

It was obvious he was blind, but what if he had other impending needs in addition to his blindness? He could have asked for anything. He could have asked for a house, a donkey, or anything else. We need to be specific when we use the key of David.

Jesus waited for his response. He said he wanted to see. Jesus touched him and healed his blindness, and his life was changed forever.

I wish there was a way to know the rest of this man's life—what he did and how he lived. I am sure he became a history maker.

May the Lord give each one of us the revelation of the Son of David. And a revelation of the throne of David, the tabernacle, and the key of David, without which the kingdom of God cannot operate on the earth.

The Throne of David

The throne of David represents the actual rulership. The throne provided the authority structure and gave the platform to execute what David heard while he was in the tabernacle. Without the throne, what he heard from God would not have been implemented or practiced. What good is it to hear from God and not have the means to execute what we heard? It will remain a good idea.

The throne gave the legal authority to accomplish in the natural what David heard from the Father during his private meetings with Him. As it is in heaven, so be it on earth. The throne is the citadel of power from whence decrees and laws are made and executed.

The throne of David is situated on Mount Zion, both on earth and in heaven. We have access to this throne and Mount Zion through Jesus. We have come by faith to the Jerusalem and the Mount Zion which are in heaven (Hebrews 12:22).

Once a decree has been made by a person or a king sitting on a throne, it becomes the law of the land. Nobody can reverse or question it. That is why the throne of David is so important, and Jesus inherited that throne. Jesus cannot rule the earth without the throne of David. The throne gives Him the proper authority structure to rule from. Otherwise, it will be like when He came to earth the first time. People didn't want to listen or believe Him, though He was their King. It won't happen like that the next time.

THE BIRTHING OF A KINGDOM NATION

The tabernacle is where heaven met earth: where the spiritual connected with the natural and heaven and earth came together in one accord. The throne gave the legal right to accomplish whatever was imparted or discussed in the tabernacle. The throne gives legal right to God and His kingdom to accomplish what they want to see happen on earth. Without the throne, it is an illegal operation.

The tabernacle is the place where everything in the natural is turned off to listen to what the Spirit is saying, where we are eager to hear from our Father. This is how we seek Him and His kingdom. It has to be personal.

In the tabernacle of Moses, we couldn't go in any time we wanted. Only when God invited and whom He invited was permitted to go into this tabernacle. The tabernacle of David is not so. You can come in anytime you have a need, or anytime you want to talk or meet with your heavenly Father. Just like we read in Hebrews 4:16, we can come boldly to the throne of grace anytime we need help from above.

David received, lived, and operated under the revelation of the new covenant. He related with God as his Father, which made God very happy because that is how He always wanted to relate with humans: as Father and children. Adam was the son of God but lost his sonship when he fell. Through Jesus Christ, God restored our sonship.

The throne represents the King, and in this case, that is Jesus Christ, the King of all kings.

He rules with mercy, truth, righteousness, and justice for all. We don't sit on any throne to rule anything or anyone right now. Jesus is the only One who is qualified to sit on David's throne because He inherited it.

The Tabernacle of David

On that day I will raise up the tabernacle of David, which has fallen down, and repair its damages; I will raise up its ruins, and rebuild it as in the days of old. (Amos 9:11)

David is the first human being who established the kingdom and the government of Christ (God) on the earth. He pitched a tent to meet with God, and the only furniture in that tent was the ark of the covenant. Whenever he needed direction or counsel from God, he went into that tent to spend time with Him.

I believe that is where he received the inspiration and the download for many of the psalms he wrote. He established a protocol for self-government, and how to rule and govern the affairs of a nation, and the earth, by partnering with God. He did not do anything unless he first sought the counsel of God.

God has always wanted to rule, reign, and govern the earth through mankind. He did not want humans to be robotic, and God does not want to impose His rule on people as a dictator does. He wants a willing vessel who will give himself or herself to Him in total surrender to do His will. That is the kind of people He is looking for. He wants each individual to choose to be ruled by Him. God found such a man in David, who will do all His will (Acts 13:22).

What was the tabernacle of David? It was not a choir with a bunch of people singing inside a tent. It was not a revival tent as we might think. It was the headquarters of the kingdom of heaven on earth. It was a private "room" or place where God and David had high-level security or governmental meetings where he received direction and counsel from the King on how to govern the affairs of the nation of Israel. It was a place like Eden, where God met with Adam.

God's government does not require a building made with expensive stones, marbles, or metals. He is not interested in the art works of man's hands or accomplishments. He wants to live with the humble and lowly in heart (Psalm 138:6). What He is looking for is a man or woman who is willing to yield to Him. Though David was a skilled warrior, his trust was not in his ability, skill, sword, or spear. His trust was in the Hands of God who taught his hands to war, and who prepared his fingers for battle (Psalm 144:1).

God is not impressed by any man-made buildings or structures, like the temple King Herod built. He built the temple, not because of his love for God and His kingdom, nor for the sake of the Jewish people, rather, he built it because of the temple tax he could collect from the Jews, which brought income to him and his government (Matthew 17:24). He also received a percentage of all the sales that took place in the temple.

That is why Jesus was so angry to see what was happening in the temple. He had to make a leash and whip them because they made the temple a den of thieves. It was supposed to be a house of prayer for all nations. And a place where nations should have been able to receive counsel from God regarding their destiny and how to govern.

The temple was supposed to be providing spiritual governance for all nations. It was meant to be a place where people from all nations could come to Jerusalem and learn the ways of God and His kingdom, and how to partner with Him to rule their nations. The priests were supposed to be teaching the people the laws of God, kingdom governance, His purpose, patterns, principles, and plans. But, instead, they were abusing and stealing from the people because they had to meet the quota King Herod demanded from them each month. Otherwise, their position and even their life was in danger.

THE GOVERNMENT OF GOD - PART 2

When the disciples showed Jesus all the architecture and the artwork of the temple Herod built, He was not impressed. He said it will be torn down to the ground and rooted out from its foundation. In the new covenant, we are the temple of God through whom He wants to govern the nations.

It is interesting to see that there were two high priests in Israel during Jesus's time. According to the law, there should have been only one at a time. One was appointed by the religious Jewish leaders, following the law of Moses, and the other one was the political appointee of Rome, the representative of Rome and Caesar (Luke 3:1-2).

David wouldn't make a move unless God told him to move and told him where and how to move. Though he may have had many flaws as a human, when it came to the things of God, he did not play any games. He did it with all of his heart, soul, mind, and strength. Whether he danced before God or wanted to find a place to offer a sacrifice, he did not spare anything. He gave Him his best. He risked his life for God and His people. He is one of the rare individuals in the Old Testament that said he loved the LORD (Psalm 18:1).

We read about the tabernacle and the throne of David in many places in the Bible. In the book of Acts alone, David is mentioned ten times. Peter preached about David on the day of Pentecost. Without David, there is no kingdom of God on the earth. Why? Because of David's revelation of the kingdom of God, God made an eternal and unconditional covenant with David and his house. It is called the sure mercies of David (Isaiah 55:3; Acts 13:34). What is the covenant that God made with David, and the sure mercies? Let us explore.

God sent His prophet and told David that when his days are over, God will establish his kingdom and his throne, and they will remain forever and ever on the earth. He will not take or remove His mercy from David and his descendants, even if they disobey or rebel against God and His purpose. He will punish and discipline them, but he will not remove His mercy from them like He removed it from the house of King Saul.

The tabernacle of David has to do with the government of God, and the throne of David is where the king sits and rules the nation. The tabernacle has to do with the reign of God, but the throne has to do with rule of man led by God.

> In mercy the throne will be established; and One will sit on it in truth, in the tabernacle of David, judging and seeking justice and hastening righteousness. (Isaiah 16:5)

The above verse tells us the purpose of the tabernacle of David. It has to do with the government of God, administering justice and righteousness. The tabernacle shows the process of being governed by God, where each individual develops a personal relationship with their heavenly Father to hear His voice and follow Him by faith through the Holy Spirit.

God promised David that he will raise up a seed after him to sit on his throne to rule the world in righteousness, justice, and peace. That Seed is Jesus Christ. This is how Jesus is known as the Son of David. When Jesus was born, He inherited the throne of David and the right to rule the house of Jacob forever and ever (Luke 1:33).

The Jews rejected Jesus and His kingdom because they couldn't understand the nature and operation of His kingdom. They only understood the nature of the kingdoms and empires of this world. Jesus's kingdom is not of this world. They wanted a big palace for their king and a huge army that would fight and kill their enemies. They wanted to sit on their king's right and left and rule with him. Jesus was not ready for such a kingdom yet.

THE GOVERNMENT OF GOD - PART 2

In God's kingdom, before we rule, we first have to die. Sometimes it is dying to the earthly attachments, ambitions, passions, and lusts. In the kingdom of God, whatever you want to receive, first you have to give it away. If you want to live in His kingdom, then first you have to give your life away (Matthew 16:25). If you want to become great in the kingdom of God, you need to become the servant of all first. It is a spiritual kingdom that runs contrary to our natural way of thinking.

If you want to be exalted, then you need to humble yourself. If you want to be rich in this kingdom, then you need to give away everything you have.

If you want to be forgiven by God, then you need to forgive those who offended you first.

If you want to be noticed and honored by people in a gathering, don't take the prominent seat; go and sit in the last row, and then the Master of Ceremonies will invite you to come forward and take the prominent seat. Then people will notice you.

In God's kingdom, blessed are those who mourn, for they shall be comforted. Blessed are the poor in spirit. In the kingdoms of this world, blessed are those who are rich and prominent.

In this kingdom of God, the King says to rejoice when you are persecuted for righteousness sake, and when people say all kinds of evil against you.

The ark of the covenant represented the presence of God. In fact, the Old Testament was all about the presence of God. In the New Testament, we don't chase the presence of God because we have access to the Person of God, and He lives inside each believer.

God dwells in us, not just His presence. We have the Person of God and the Holy Spirit in us because we are His temple (1 Corinthians

3:16; 6:19). We don't just "feel" the Holy Spirit once in a while, but we carry Him inside of us 24/7.

This is an important truth to understand because there are so many in the church world today who still seek or chase the "presence" of God because they are not aware of the Person of God dwelling inside of them. They borrow or quote some verses or experiences of people in the old covenant and get stuck with it. They don't understand how God relates with us in the new covenant. They are not aware of the new covenant realities that have been made available to us through Christ. The majority of the songs we sing are based on old covenant theology.

We don't need to build an ark of the covenant and a tabernacle like David did. Our ark of the covenant is Jesus Christ, the Author and Finisher of our faith, who said He will never leave us nor forsake us. He lives in us. Christ in us the hope of glory.

Jesus said His sheep hear His voice. We walk by faith and not by what we feel. Music was an important factor in the old covenant because the Person of God couldn't dwell with humans, nor could the presence of God.

Under the old covenant, the presence of God manifested only when a certain type of music played or when special sacrifices were offered. In the new covenant, we live with God and He lives with us 24/7. In the new covenant, we offer our bodies as a living sacrifice (Romans 12:1). We don't see such musical performances anywhere in the New Testament. What we see in the churches today has been adopted from the western pop music culture.

The name David is mentioned 56 times in the New Testament, including ten times in the book of Acts. Not even one time is he mentioned in relation to music, singing, or dancing. It was all in relation to his revelation of the kingdom of God. Unfortunately, what

THE GOVERNMENT OF GOD - PART 2

we hear about David in the church world today is about his singing, dancing, and Goliath. Lord, have mercy!

Don't misunderstand me. There is music in every kingdom. Wherever a king is, there should be music and joy. There is music in heaven. Whenever a head of state or king arrives, there is music to receive and celebrate them. It's a kingdom or royal protocol.

The tabernacle of David represents how the government of God works on the earth in relation to humans. It shows how God wants to reign over and through His people. When we think of government, we think of huge buildings and structures, with one man or woman on the top of it all. That's what people built in the name of God. Or to make a name for themselves, as they did with the tower of Babel.

God was not in any of these things. When certain individuals, structures, systems, and buildings become our main focus, we miss God and His Spirit. That is not God's kingdom. The Bible calls it the way of the gentiles.

> Thus says the Lord: "Do not learn the way of the Gentiles; do not be dismayed at the signs of heaven, for the Gentiles are dismayed at them." (Jeremiah 10:2)

> These twelve Jesus sent out and commanded them, saying: "Do not go into the way of the Gentiles, and do not enter a city of the Samaritans." (Matthew 10:5)

What was Jesus talking about when he said not to go into the way of the gentiles, and do not enter a city of the Samaritans? We thought He was telling them not to travel on a particular road where the gentiles are living, and not to share the good news of the kingdom with any gentiles or Samaritans, right?

That cannot be so because Jesus Himself told them to go to the end of the earth, and He Himself shared and revealed Himself as the Messiah to a Samaritan woman. He wanted to go through Samaria to preach to them, but they wouldn't receive Him. He is not talking about physical roads or individuals here, but systems and ways of operation.

We need to interpret scriptures with other scriptures. In Jeremiah 10:2, God specifically said, "*Do not learn* the way of the Gentiles." He is talking about their ways of living and doing things. The way of the gentile is contrary to the way of the kingdom of God. We need to be careful with this.

Jesus also warned His disciples about leadership styles and other ways and spirits of the gentiles. Trying to build something for Him, like Peter wanted to do on the Mount of Transfiguration, is not God's way. As they went to do their kingdom assignment, He told them to be careful and to not follow the ways of the gentiles and try to build God's kingdom like the cities built by the Samaritans. There is a spiritual implication to this instruction given by Him.

Samaritans took what Jewish people had and tried to duplicate it in Samaria. They are half-Jewish and half-gentile. They established their own worship systems, a different place of worship (another mountain other than Jerusalem). What they had was fake, and Jesus said, 'do not be like them.'

When you start doing your kingdom assignment, do not follow the way of the gentiles or build things like the cities of Samaria. Do not fake things or build things just because they sound good. Make sure you follow the ways of God. There are fake signs, wonders, and false advertisements people do in the name of God.

They use the name of Jesus Christ and His kingdom to build cults and gentile kingdoms; and they colonize nations and build big ministries and mega churches. That is not the way of the kingdom but the way of the gentiles. Many things we see in the church today are the way of the gentiles: the style of music, church growth techniques, leadership styles, etc.

> And when the ten heard *it,* they were greatly displeased with the two brothers. But Jesus called them to *Himself* and said, "You know that the rulers of the Gentiles lord it over them, and those who are great exercise authority over them. Yet it shall not be so among you; but whoever desires to become great among you, let him be your servant." (Matthew 20:24-26)

People have built cathedrals, palaces, thrones, monuments, organizations, ministries, and empires all in the name of God. But they are not God's kingdom or His way. They are the ways of the gentiles and the cities of Samaria. They are counterfeit.

God wants to keep things simple, but holy and undefiled. His ways are easy, but they are deep. An eagle can see it from the sky, but a human may miss it from close proximity. When we understand the tabernacle that David erected, we will understand how God wants to govern His people. He wants each one to have a relationship with Him, and to hear His voice and do what He says. This is the ultimate form of self-government.

Everyone won't be able to hear God at the same level. So, at times, we all need each other. Sometimes we need to hear through others what God is speaking. Each of us needs to mature and grow in our relationship with our heavenly Father, and hear and follow His voice.

David had a habit of going to God when He had a problem or situation. That is why he set up a personal tabernacle, and it is where he spent time with God. Each time he was at a crossroad or faced a battle or crisis, he would go to God to hear what He would say about it. Then, when he heard from God, he went out and did exactly what he heard.

Before David went to fight his enemies, he always went to God to receive a battle strategy. God is the ultimate strategist and warrior, and no one can defeat Him. That is why David never lost a battle in his life. He followed God's direction every step of the way.

Sometimes God sent a prophet to David who spoke to him the word of the Lord. We all need that from time to time. There is nothing wrong with hearing the voice of God through other fellow believers. We cannot be stubborn and say we only hear from God directly and won't receive His instructions from others. If we do that, we will get into pride, rebellion, and independence, which God hates.

This tabernacle was different and separate from the tabernacle that Moses built. One unique thing about this tabernacle was that there was only one piece of furniture in it. It was the ark of the covenant. The tabernacle of Moses had seven pieces of furniture in it, which represented different things in the spirit.

> So they brought the ark of the LORD, and set it in its place in the midst of the tabernacle that David had erected for it. Then David offered burnt offerings and peace offerings before the LORD. (2 Samuel 6:17)

The tabernacle Moses built was for a different purpose. People couldn't go into it. Even Moses could go only when the Lord invited him. In the tabernacle of David, it was not so. David could go into it anytime he wanted to meet with the Lord. It represented the new covenant and was how God always wanted it.

God wants to dwell with us. That is why Jesus said when we pray, go into the room and close the door because this is between God and us. It is supposed to be a private meeting. The Father wants each of His children to come to Him when they need Him—to hear from Him and to be loved by Him. Each of us is special to Him and has a unique place in His heart.

> But you, when you pray, go into your room, and when you have shut your door, pray to your Father who *is* in the secret *place;* and your Father who sees in secret will reward you openly. (Matthew 6:6)

> But when you pray, go into your most private room, close the door and pray to your Father who is in secret, and your Father who sees [what is done] in secret will reward you. (Matthew 6:6, AMP)

Jesus is introducing the same system to us that David followed in his life. Each one of us is supposed to meet with God our Father in private or in secret, to hear His voice and to receive direction from Him. Jesus said to go into a room instead of a tabernacle.

We don't see Jesus praying with His disciples. If He did that, they wouldn't have asked Him to teach them how to pray. They could have watched Him and learned. He didn't pray to impress them of His spirituality. He kept it as a private business between Him and the Father. God considers prayer a private meeting between you and your heavenly Father.

When the Bible talks about prayer, the majority of the time, it mentions it as a private matter. There is nothing wrong with praying with others. We see in the book of Acts the church prayed for Peter when he was put in prison.

Private prayer time is the most important thing in our life. Again, prayer is not telling God what to do or presenting Him with our long list of needs. Prayer is the most intimate thing you will ever do with God. One of the most important components of prayer is being real and honest with Him. Don't put on all those religious postures, vocabularies, and mannerisms to impress God or to get His attention. What attracts God is our honest heart and pure intentions.

God has a place in His heart for each one of us. This is the place Jesus said He was going to prepare for us and then come back to us (to the disciples in a little while) in John 14. It was not any mansion in heaven as we think of it, or as the religious spirit told us. Jesus is the way to the Father, and He is the way to the holy of holies—He is the Door.

We lost our Father because of the fall. We did not know how to approach Him. He could not relate with us as sons and daughters. Jesus came to restore that relationship. He came to show us the way back to our Father's heart, our eternal place in Him.

You might ask, 'Don't we have enough people already running around saying God told them this and God told them that?' The majority of these people did not hear from God at all. They had an inspired thought or imagination that originated from their own desires and needs. First of all, God won't tell them to tell you what you must do or not. That is not their responsibility. If they heard from God, then what they say should bear witness with what is already in your spirit man.

Also, if what they say is not in line with God's written Word, then run from it. Don't believe or trust the people who walk around and say they carry extra or special revelation that is not written in God's Word. In that case also, run from such people. Don't believe them when they say they went to heaven and came back with a special word that contradicts the written Word. Or if someone says an angel appeared to them and gave them a special message—they are false and demon spirits pretending to be angels of light.

Third, if what they say is not in alignment with God's eternal purpose of establishing His kingdom and will on earth, then don't receive it. If it permanently alters or deviates from what God already told you, or His calling on your life, run and don't look back.

If what they say is causing division and strife among the people, then they are sowing discord among the brethren and they should be avoided. "Now I urge you, brethren, note those who cause divisions and offenses, contrary to the doctrine which you learned, and avoid them." (Romans 16:17)

> Now I plead with you, brethren, by the name of our Lord Jesus Christ, that you all speak the same thing, and *that* there be no divisions among you, but *that* you be perfectly joined together in the same mind and in the same judgment. (1 Corinthians 1:10)

This is why the service and ministry of the fivefold gifts are very important to the body of Christ. Their job is to teach and train each believer on how to connect with their heavenly Father individually. We all start as newborn babes, we all need training and equipping on how to live in God's kingdom and on how to relate with Him as our Father and on how to hear His voice.

A parent's goal is not to keep his or her child dependent on them forever. The purpose of parenting is for the child to grow and mature and be able to do things on their own. No parent wants their children depending on them for the rest of their lives and living with them in the family house.

Instead of doing this, self-appointed or immature fivefold ministry gifts draw people to themselves and keep them attached to them. They became like the gentile leaders, lording it over people and expecting their submission and obedience. They treat God's people as second-class citizens and, in turn, treat themselves as a super holy or hyper-spiritual gang leader. They think they are the only ones who are called by God and hear from Him. They will not teach or tell a believer in Christ that they are called by God to do something specific in the kingdom.

These leaders won't teach people to hear from God for themselves. They want the people to depend on them to hear God for them and keep paying their dues for their spiritual food. These saints remain spiritual babies for the rest of their lives. This happens because of the immaturity or ignorance of the ministers who follow the Babylonian pyramid leadership style. They abuse and take the saints of God for granted.

Instead of training and releasing them, they keep the saints of God as slaves. They are worried about their survival, without knowing that if they would release the people to do what God has called them to do, they would be blessed and God would honor them and give them increase.

To be honest with you, one of the main problems, and the reason the body of Christ is malfunctioning, immature, and ineffective is because of these self-appointed fivefold ministers. They keep dividing the body to build their own ministries and start new churches. They are not building God's kingdom; they are using God's people to build their own little kingdoms. They are the main hindrance to the kingdom of God manifesting on the earth. I left the "ministry" that I was building and came into God's kingdom, and the rest is history.

The book of Revelation is the conclusion of everything, especially the last two chapters. In Revelation 21:3-4 we read,

> And I heard a loud voice from heaven saying, "Behold, the tabernacle of God is with men, and He will dwell with them, and they shall be His people. God Himself will be with

them and be their God. And God will wipe away every tear from their eyes; there shall be no more death, nor sorrow, nor crying. There shall be no more pain, for the former things have passed away."

We read about the tabernacle of God here again. It's been God's desire to dwell with us and among us. David had a revelation of this eternal tabernacle in the spirit and applied it to his own life. He made it a reality in his life.

David established the kingdom and handed it over to his son Solomon. Solomon means 'the son of peace.' He is a type of Christ in the Old Testament. David represents the Father, and he handed over the kingdom to his son, just like the Father gave His kingdom to His Son Jesus.

That's why Jesus said, "It is your Father's good pleasure to give you the kingdom (Luke 12:32). In another place, He said, "And I bestow upon you a kingdom, just as My Father bestowed *one* upon Me (Luke 22:29).

When we study the reign of Solomon, and the kingdom and reign of Christ, we see many similarities. If we are to understand the reign of Christ, we need to see the pattern in the Old Testament. The sad thing is that Solomon's reign didn't last long, but Christ's reign will last forever and ever.

> David established and gave the kingdom to Solomon, his son. The Father gave the kingdom to His Son, Jesus.

> David made sure all his enemies are defeated and brought to his son's foot stool.

The Father told the Son to sit at His right hand until He makes all His enemies His footstool. This particular verse from Psalm 110:1 is quoted seven times in the New Testament for a specific reason; it needs to be fulfilled before Jesus comes back. In Hebrews 10:12-13, we read that Jesus has been waiting for this to happen and now it's been over two thousand years. Until this happens, He will not get up from where He is seated to do anything else.

That is why in Acts 2 we read about God pouring out His Spirit upon all flesh, and then in Acts 9:11, about the rebuilding of the tabernacle of David. God wants all His children to hear His voice and to be led by His Spirit. This is how the government of God should work.

The Key of David

> "And to the angel of the church in Philadelphia write, 'These things says He who is holy, He who is true, "He who has the key of David, He who opens and no one shuts, and shuts and no one opens." (Revelation 3:7)

David was a man after God's own heart who did all His will (Acts 13:22). Most people have only heard about the David and Goliath story, or his dance before the Lord.

Most have never heard about the Son of David, the tabernacle, or the throne and the key of David. In these four components lie the entire government of God and it's process.

The specialty of the key of David is that if you use it to open anything, no one can close it. If you use it to close anything, no one can open it. This speaks of legislation or jurisdiction. It is the same principle Jesus mentioned in Matthew 16:19 with regard to binding and loosing, or forbidding and permitting what happens on the earth. It's one of the keys of God's kingdom.

Why does David's key hold such authority in the spirit and in God's kingdom? Remember that everything in the universe revolves around God and His kingdom. When a human enters into partnership with God in relation to any of His kingdom assignments, that person becomes unstoppable. That person carries and represents the authority of heaven.

No enemy or force is powerful enough to stop or destroy that person, though they can destroy themselves. God entrusts them with His authority to destroy any enemy force. This can be used positively or negatively.

People can get into their dark side and use this authority to destroy themselves or others. That's what happened to Lucifer. He held such authority, power, and splendor, but he corrupted it because of wealth, wisdom, beauty, and pride.

Jeremiah was another individual who held such authority. He could speak a word over a king or a nation, and that became their future (Jeremiah 1:10). Elijah was another person who could close the heavens with his words, and it wouldn't rain until he spoke again.

What exactly is the key of David? The whole kingdom, power, glory, and authority works according to revelation: revelation of who God is and what He possess. You have access to the kingdom and everything in it through revelation. Revelation is the master key that unlocks and gives access to everything else in God's kingdom.

That is why we need the spirit of wisdom and revelation to operate and live in the kingdom of God. Without it, nothing will make sense.

The key of David is the revelation of the kingdom of God and His government. That key is the revelation of our sonship in God's kingdom. A son means one who has a Father. In this case, God Almighty becomes our Father. David was one of the rare people who operated in sonship under the old covenant (Psalm 27:10; 68:5).

THE BIRTHING OF A KINGDOM NATION

Praise is part of the key of David. We, as a church, have exaggerated that aspect more than necessary and neglected the weightier aspects. Access to God and His throne is another dimension of this key. Revelation of the wealth and riches that God's kingdom possesses is another dimension of this key.

The key of David is the revelation of the kingdom of God and its King, the Messiah. Peter received this revelation in Matthew chapter 16. When Jesus was on the earth, few people understood who He really was. There were only two other people who received this revelation while Jesus was on the earth. One was the woman at the well, and the second was the blind man, Bartimaeus. It is important to note that God uses the most unlikely people to accomplish His purposes.

That is why the Bible says that God chooses the foolish things of this world to confound the wise. David wrote many messianic psalms. He received a revelation of not only the kingdom of God, but the Messiah, who is going to rule that kingdom.

The key of David represents the following dimensions of revelation:

1. Revelation of the kingdom of God

2. Revelation of the Messiah—the King of the kingdom

3. Revelation of the throne room of God—Come boldly to the throne of grace. That is what David did in his tabernacle. He went to God directly and related with Him as his Father.

4. Revelation of dominion—This key opens what no man can close, and closes what no one can open.

5. Revelation of accessing heaven and making it a reality on earth. A believer has access to heaven at any time.

6. Revelation of the treasury and resources of the kingdom

In any kingdom or building, each room will have a door and a key for that door. Then there is a master key that only the master holds, which opens all the doors. The key of David is a master key that opens many things in God's kingdom for a believer.

> The key of the house of David I will lay on his shoulder; So he shall open, and no one shall shut; And he shall shut, and no one shall open. (Isaiah 22:22)

I believe now you have an idea of what the government of God should look like. May the Lord help each one of us to practice what is written here.

Chapter 10

The Twelve Components of a Kingdom Nation

> In the middle of its street, and on either side of the river, was the tree of life, which bore twelve fruits, each tree yielding its fruit every month. The leaves of the tree were for the healing of the nations. (Revelation 22:2)

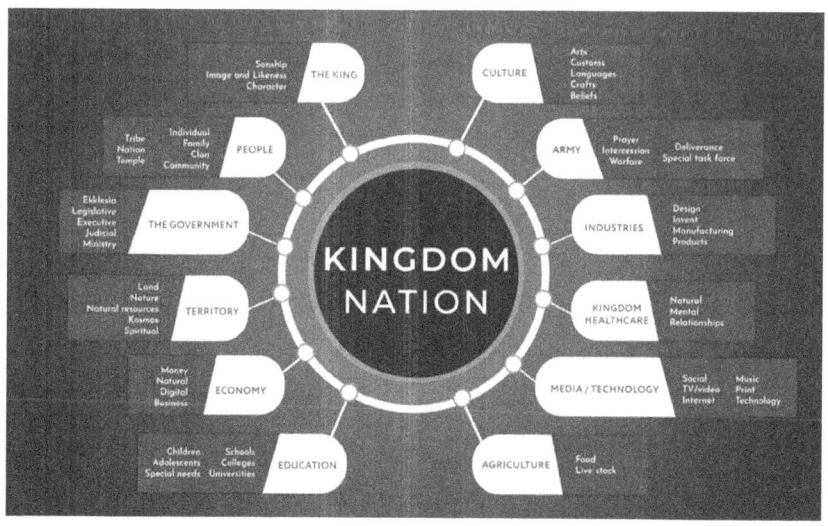

THE BIRTHING OF A KINGDOM NATION

Everything God does in relation to His kingdom is connected to a particular number, especially when it comes to His government; that number is twelve. Twelve is the number of Kingdom Government. That is why there are twelve tribes in the nation of Israel. In order to start the new Kingdom Nation, Jesus again chose twelv men. God always follows the pattern and principles He established in His Word.

The number twelve is mentioned ten times in the book of Revelation. From each tribe of Israel, twelve thousand people will be sealed. Twelve thousand is one thousand times twelve. The new Jerusalem is embodied with number twelve. It has twelve gates with twelve angels at each gate. The wall of the city has twelve foundations. The size of the city is twelve thousand furloughs, with equal length, height, and breadth.

The twelve gates are made of twelve pearls. Then, in the last chapter of Revelation, we read about the Tree of Life that bears twelve fruits. Then we read about twenty-four elders.

How are we going to offer solutions for the world's problems? How are we going to bring healing to the nations? How are we going to transform our existing nations to become kingdom nations? Whatever problem this earth faces, the kingdom of God has the solution; in fact, it is the solution.

That is why God the Father sent His only Son with the message of the kingdom. The gospel of the kingdom was the only message the Father authorized His Son Jesus to preach. So when Jesus sent out His disciples, the only message He authorized them to preach was the message of the kingdom.

The reason we have problems in every nation is because we have been operating without the kingdom of God. The reason the systems

THE TWELVE COMPONENTS OF A KINGDOM NATION

of this world are falling apart is because they are counterfeit. When that which is real manifests, people will understand the difference between the fake and the authentic. God never intended this earth to function without His kingdom. When an aspect of this earth attempts to function without God's kingdom, there will be problems—that aspect will certainly malfunction.

If the governments of our nations are to be healed, the solution is Kingdom Government. If the economy of this world is to be healed, Kingdom Economy needs to manifest. If our bodies and minds are to be healthy, then Kingdom Healthcare needs to manifest.

When the education system of this world produces slaves, we need Kingdom Education to liberate people to fulfill their God-given purpose and sonship. We need to take back the manufacturing sector from the enemy's hands by introducing kingdom industries.

If we want to produce healthy foods that are good for our body and mind, we need Kingdom Agriculture in every nation. That is why Jesus came and gave us the kingdom. Until now, we have not known what to do with the kingdom God has given us. It is time to manifest His kingdom on the earth. To do that, we are starting first with the Kingdom Nation. We must launch a prototype nation for other nations to copy and follow.

In this chapter, I want to mention the twelve components of a kingdom nation. We need to manifest them in our nations, based on each of our individual callings. God has been raising up people from every nation, and they are being trained and equipped to understand the kingdom and how to manifest it.

We currently have believers from more than thirty countries who have joined together to form this kingdom nation. If you are reading this book, and you are not part of this kingdom nation and would like to join, please send us an email or contact us through one of our social media platforms or visit www.RegnoEthnos.com.

Twenty-Four Men and Twelve Tribes

Why would God want twelve tribes and twelve disciples or apostles? Twelve is an important number in God's kingdom. It is the number of kingdom government. Whatever God does in relation to His kingdom government has a connection to the number twelve or its multiplication.

God's kingdom has twelve major components. You may have read about this in a previous book or heard me teach on it before. The nation of Israel had twelve tribes, and each tribe was uniquely anointed and graced by God to fulfill a specific role in the overall function of the nation. I believe that is the reason God wanted the twelve tribes.

That is also the reason Jesus selected twelve apostles to start this new nation called the Ekklesia. The same principle that we saw in the Old Testament was followed in the New Testament. Remember, God always follows a specific pattern in everything He does. It is our duty to search out and discover those patterns and principles, and apply them.

God wants everything in heaven to manifest on the earth. As it is in heaven, so should it be on earth. There are twenty-four elders in heaven that are a part of God's governing body. There were one hundred and twenty in the upper room, waiting for the arrival of the Holy Spirit—the Governor General of God's kingdom. Three thousand people came into the kingdom to form the Ekklesia on the day of Pentecost. The Ekklesia is the governing body of Christ's kingdom on earth. These are some of the multiplications of the number twelve mentioned in the Bible.

That's why I said that anything that has to do with God's kingdom government and nation is connected to the number twelve. That is why we will follow the same pattern God established in forming this kingdom nation. God is raising up twelve tribes, each one specializing in a different area and component of the kingdom for the overall function of the nation.

All twelve components of the kingdom were present in the garden, and that's why there are twelve tribes in the nation of Israel, and then twelve apostles.

Each of those tribes was uniquely graced by God to be the head of each component of the kingdom, and each one of them excelled in its particular area in the Kingdom Nation.

Each tribe was also divided into different clans and then families; each clan and family fulfilled a unique role in the overall function of that tribe and the nation as a whole.

For example, each component of the kingdom is too big and complicated for one person to manage. The component of economy is made of many subcategories like business, banking, and money, both fiat and digital. Education is complicated. We need people who are trained to teach all ages of children. Because there will be children with special needs, one system or size won't fit all in the kingdom.

Another component is agriculture; it is too big for one person or family to manage. That specific tribe needs to farm and produce all kinds of food that grows in different seasons and locations, and in different weather patterns. All trees and plants and fruits won't grow everywhere. Different families and clans will focus on producing different kinds of crops.

Each believer in Christ belongs to one of these tribes, and each tribe is sub-divided into clans and families. Each component is so huge that it takes more than one person or clan to manage. Remember, each of the tribes in the nation of Israel started with one individual. They grew and multiplied and then became a nation. It was the same process we are in right now.

God always starts with an individual. It was just Adam in the beginning, and now there are close to eight billion people on earth. One of the reasons the church is not effective is because people cannot find a community where they feel they belong. We cannot put everyone together and hope they find their place. All seeds won't grow together. Each requires a particular soil and environment.

Now let's explore the twelve components of the Kingdom Nation and how we can bring healing to the nations by fulfilling what each of us is called to do.

1. The King

Psalm 10:16 says, "The LORD is King forever and ever." His kingdom is an everlasting kingdom, and his dominion is from generation to generation. There is not a time or generation where God ceased from being a King and His kingdom stopped ruling the earth. There is a misconception among the body of Christ that Jesus, or God, will only reign on the earth during the millennial reign. That is not true.

The kingdom age began on earth the day it was created. God created the earth to establish His kingdom. He never took a break from His purpose. The only thing delaying His plan is that the people He created got distracted or were kidnapped by another king and kingdom. He has been waiting patiently for us for a very long time. The moment we align ourselves with God's purpose for our lives, things on earth will turn for good and in the right direction. Until then, things will continue to go from bad to worse. There is no point in blaming God or the devil. God gave us the authority to decide what needs to happen on the earth.

> And the Lord shall be King over all the earth. In that day it shall be— "The Lord *is* one," And His name one. (Zechariah 14:9)

The above prophecy has not been fulfilled yet. May it be fulfilled in our lifetime.

> Yours, O Lord, *is* the greatness, The power and the glory, The victory and the majesty; for all *that is* in heaven and in earth *is Yours;* Yours *is* the kingdom, O Lord, And You are exalted as head over all. (1 Chronicles 29:11)

We are created as kings and priests. It is our responsibility to manifest God and His kingdom on the earth. There are people who are called to be in government. Make sure you are called to be there; don't go in there just because it is a good idea.

2. Kingdom Territory

No kingdom can survive without a territory. The territory the Lord entrusted us with is the earth. Earth is God's kingdom territory, and we are supposed to steward it faithfully. Instead, we have been squandering and destroying this planet. We were created for the earth, rather than the earth being created for us.

It is interesting to notice that, several times, the Lord says the earth belongs to Him. Exodus 19:5 says, "Now therefore, if you will indeed obey My voice and keep My covenant, then you shall be a special treasure to Me above all people; for all the earth *is* Mine." (see also Psalm 24:1; 1 Corinthians 10:26 & 28).

In the Old Testament, the Lord told the people of Israel that if they do not take care of the land by remaining faithful to Him, they will lose the land—He will punish them by sending them to captivity.

THE BIRTHING OF A KINGDOM NATION

In the New Testament, Jesus shared many parables about stewardship of the property and resources He gave to us.

In the book of Revelation, we read that when Jesus comes back, He will destroy those who destroyed the earth.

> The nations were angry, and Your wrath has come, And the time of the dead, that they should be judged, and that You should reward Your servants the prophets and the saints, And those who fear Your name, small and great, And should destroy those who destroy the earth. (Revelation 11:18)

One of the main differences between developed nations and underdeveloped nations, that I have noticed, is how they take care of the land. In underdeveloped nations, they don't value or take care of the land. They abuse and misuse it for their benefit. In developed nations, the land is well kept and taken care of.

The King is happy when we take good care of His kingdom property, and then He will bless us and the land. When the land is blessed, people will also be blessed. We depend on the land for our survival. Everything we use and need comes from the land. We were created to take care of the land and to see God's kingdom and will accomplished in every aspect of our lives.

God can only bless what we maximize and put to good use. God promised to bless the fruit of our body. One of the fruits of our body is the works we do with our hands. Sometimes laziness and unproductivity cause us to look for a miracle. Many Christians are waiting for God to do what He told them to do.

When God comes to bless them, He notices there is no seed planted in the ground. The ground is not tilled. There are bushes and thistles everywhere. They are sleeping by folding their hands between their legs (Proverbs 24:30-32). Then when He looks at the heathen living next door to a Christian, He notices their land tilled, seeds are sown, and it is well taken care of. He blesses them, and they become productive and rich, while the Christians are running from one revival meeting to the next looking for a miracle.

God created Adam to take care of the land. When He called Abraham, it was about the earth and the land. Jesus said, "Blessed are the meek, for they shall inherit the earth" (Matthew 5:5). Every Kingdom Nation citizen should own and steward at least one piece of land in their respective country, for the kingdom of God.

As kingdom citizens, we should be the largest land owners. Without land or territory, there is no kingdom.

3. The People

People are the backbone of any nation or kingdom. The more productive people we have in a country, the more prosperous that nation will become. The Bible says that God created humans male and female. There are only two genders authorized by God. Ever since the fall, confusion came between male and female and their different roles and functions in society. They began to fight each other for domination and control.

Males began to dominate females, and then females in return started to rebel against the males. As a result, machoism and feminism were birthed. What we see happening now in families and in our society between males and females is not what God intended.

We are living in a time when it is hard to find a real man or woman. We have men acting like women and women trying to be like men. There is a confusion of identity and roles that men and women are supposed to fulfill in a society. Male and female, men and women, are still the idea of the Creator.

THE BIRTHING OF A KINGDOM NATION

The reason God chose twelve men to be the head of the nation of Israel and twelve men as the apostles to establish the new nation called Ekklesia, is not because God is partial toward men and does not love women. Men and women were created by God to fulfill different roles in life. They are not created to do the same thing.

Men and women are wired differently. Their emotional needs are different. They are physically, emotionally, and sexually different. Though they are equal in the spirit, they have different emotional, physical, and spiritual capacities and needs. Only when we put both of them together will we get the complete picture, and then God will be able to fulfill His purpose for the earth through us.

Male and female were not created to dominate or compete with each other. They were created to work together as one: one body, one unit, one spirit. Remember all those twenty-four men I mentioned above came to this world through women. Without women they wouldn't be born, and without women they couldn't fulfill their purpose on the earth either.

So, my precious and honorable ladies that are reading this book, you don't need to become like a man, or do what men do, to feel accepted or significant. Just being a woman and fulfilling your God-given role is the most powerful thing you can do for God and His kingdom. It is not any less important than what men are doing. Our roles are different, but they are equally important in fulfilling our Father's assignment on the earth.

Men are builders and fighters by nature. That's how they provide for and protect their women, children, and their nation. The feminine, nurturing, caring, affectionate, and birthing (not just children but the purposes of God) nature of a woman is even more powerful. When you put them together, you get the most unstoppable force on earth.

For the establishment and proper function of the Kingdom Nation, we need to understand the different roles men and women ought to play. There is no room for fights and schisms. We need to submit to God's order and design. We need to go back to God's original design for men and women as it was in the Garden of Eden.

What makes a woman attractive to a man is the feminine qualities she possesses. The more feminine a woman is, the more she becomes attractive to a man. This is sound advice to those precious and smart ladies that are out there who can't find a man. A man is not impressed by your religiosity either. What a man needs is your feminine energy and capacity. That is what gives him fulfillment.

When I say feminine qualities, what do I mean by that? I don't mean the way you dress and how much of your body you display to the public. That is prostituting your body. The kind of man you attract by showing your body parts is not the kind of man you want to build a life with. And if a woman tries to draw a man by showing her body parts, that's not the kind of woman you want to build a life with either. In such cases, men come to you because of mere lust. What I mean by feminine qualities is the inherent beauty of a woman's heart and the nature God put in them.

You don't need to do anything special to become a woman or to become feminine; these qualities are already in you. You don't need to attach any artificial eye lashes, long and sharp nails like Dracula, or supersize your breasts or buttocks to look feminine. These kinds of beauty tips come from the Babylonian system and are not of God's kingdom.

> Do not let your adornment be *merely* outward—arranging the hair, wearing gold, or putting on *fine* apparel— rather *let it be* the hidden person of the heart, with the incorruptible

beauty of a gentle and quiet spirit, which is very precious in the sight of God. (1 Peter 3:3-4)

The Bible says that charm is deceitful and beauty is vain or will fade away, but a woman who fears the LORD will be praised (Proverbs 31:30). We live in a world where a woman's body is used as an icon for advertisements, and outward beauty (her shape and how she looks) is praised more than the heart and character. Women were not created to drive their family or to dominate men.

If a woman tries to rule over a man, she is breaking God's order and operating under the curse (Genesis 3:16). A woman needs to yield in order to receive the seed from a man. This principle is the same in both the spiritual and in the natural. They are created to work alongside their men to build God's kingdom.

In the same way, what makes a man attractive to a woman is his masculinity. This is how God designed and created us. A real woman is not impressed by an expensive car or the size and shape of the body parts of a male. The more masculine a man becomes, the more women will want his attention.

When I say masculinity, I don't mean the physical appearance of a male body alone. Masculinity, or manhood, is much more than a physical body or muscles. Though muscles and being in good shape are admirable, it is the courage, character, and capacity of a man to rule, govern, build, manage, cultivate, protect, provide, and at the same time, love sacrificially, as Christ loves the church, and care for his family and the world God created.

Men need to make sure they don't dominate women or treat them like a commodity or a sex object, but as partakers and heirs of the same grace and promises in Christ Jesus. They are queens in God's kingdom. There is nothing more beautiful to watch on earth than when a man and a woman are joined together by the Lord and become one, and understand their functions and specific roles, to accomplish His kingdom purpose without competing and dominating. This is rare to find.

This is what needs to happen through marriage, and that is the purpose of it. But most get married for the wrong reasons and out of ignorance. The majority of people have been wounded in many ways, and their wounds and defects irritate their partner rather than motivate them. Sometimes it takes people reaching forty to forty-five years of age to gain some kind of common sense about life. By that time, many get stuck with the wrong person or get divorced and become frustrated about life. The key is not to give up on life and on your relationship. Keep moving forward.

Because of the misunderstanding and misrepresentation of both genders, we have created a mess on earth, and the battle between the genders continues. I believe both genders are equally responsible for the dilemma we have created. There needs to be a reconciliation between genders and acceptance of the roles each has played to get where we are today. If we can do that, it will be the greatest favor we could do for the future generations. May the Lord help us do this.

Neither male nor female need to compete for dominance. This is demonically inspired, and it is part of the curse. We are not under the curse anymore. Sometimes people use the scripture from Galatians out of context saying there is no difference between a male and female or a Jew or a gentile. That verse is talking about salvation through Jesus Christ and the forgiveness of sins. Whether we are male or female, or Jew or gentile, we all need Jesus because there is only one way to the Father.

Of course there is a difference between a male and a female and between a Jew and a gentile. God created male and female differently, as I mentioned above. In God's grand scheme, Jewish people have their own function and role that is different from that of a gentile. We are one in Christ, but different at the same time. It is a mystery, similar to the mystery of the union between a husband and wife that Paul wrote about in Ephesians 5:31-32.

We need kingdom families to accomplish God's kingdom purpose on the earth. And we need to come out of what our culture has taught us about men and women. We need to go back to God's original design and what He intended for how a man and woman are supposed to function. Without getting this right, we won't be able to get anything else right.

Just because someone is born a male or female doesn't mean they will become a man or a woman automatically, just like no one becomes a doctor or a pilot without going to school first. The reason there is gender confusion and the identity crisis is because we are not following God's training program on how to become a man or a woman in His kingdom. God instituted this system in the book of Genesis to train Adam and Eve to become a man and a woman, then a husband and a wife, and then a father and a mother.

There is an excellent book we published called *Kingdom Family*, which talks about how God trained Adam and Eve and took them through this process. It is the blueprint for humanity. We need to implement this training program in every church around the world.

My question to those men who can't find a woman is this; are you exemplifying the qualities of a man? When you display your masculinity, you will automatically attract women to you.

God didn't create women to drive the family or to rule over men. That is why nothing happened to Adam or to Eve until Adam ate the fruit. Their purpose is to come alongside of men to accomplish God's kingdom purpose on the earth. That's why God called them a "help mate."

Men shouldn't rule over women either. They are supposed to stand together side by side. In the Old Testament, it was considered a curse to have a woman ruler (Isaiah 3:12). Paul alluded to the same principle in the New Testament when He said he doesn't permit a woman to have spiritual authority over a man (1 Timothy 2:12). It doesn't mean women cannot teach or preach.

It was to a woman (Samaritan woman in John 4:28) that Jesus revealed Himself as the Messiah for the first time. Also, it was to a woman that He appeared for the first time after His resurrection. She brought the good news of His resurrection to His disciples. That does not mean she was authorized to go and appoint the next apostle to fill Judas's place. Women aren't inferior to men in any way—in quality or in essence. They were both created to fulfill different roles in the kingdom of God.

4. Kingdom Economy

God's people have been used by the enemy to build his kingdom. Their skills, time, potential, and money have been used by the enemy. This must stop. We say we give the tithe, the ten percent to the church, but we don't realize what we do with the ninety percent. That ninety percent goes to the kingdom of darkness to sponsor its agendas. The bills we pay and the products and services we buy and use are owned and operated by the ungodly.

Sadly, the ten percent we give to the church also ends back up in the Babylonian system. The church has bills to pay, and when pastors get paid, they also go back into the world to buy food and products, and use services. Unfortunately, one hundred percent of our money and wealth is being used to build and sustain the kingdom of darkness, while the kingdom of God remains desolate and in ruin, and God's people live in bondage to Egypt and Babylon.

THE BIRTHING OF A KINGDOM NATION

Then God's people wonder why many of them are sick and broke, and why God is not helping them or doing any miracles for them. Remember, when the people of God were in Egypt, serving Pharaoh and building his kingdom, God did not do any miracles for them. They were sick and broke, and there was no miraculous provision of manna from heaven.

Only when they left Egypt to build God's kingdom, did He become their Protector and Provider. God refuses to interact and help humans outside of His kingdom purpose and context. That is why Jesus told us to seek His kingdom and His righteousness first, and then all the things we need will be added to us.

What if there was a financial system put in place to retain, manage, and multiply the wealth and money of God's people? That is what we need to do as a Kingdom Nation. As a Kingdom Nation, one of the first things we need to build is an economy. Any nation is only as strong as its economy.

That is why God put it in our hearts to start a Kingdom Family Bank. One of the first things God established for the nation of Israel and the early church was their economy. When the people of God left Egypt, God told them through Moses to borrow jewelry made of gold and other precious metals and stones. He told them to plunder the Egyptians.

The wealth they brought from Egypt was the foundation, or the capital fund, which was used later to build the nation of Israel and to build the tabernacle. One of the first things that was established in the early church was also economy or a kingdom bank. Believers sold a portion of their possessions and brought it and laid it at the feet of the apostles. Then they distributed that wealth to meet the needs of the believers.

THE TWELVE COMPONENTS OF A KINGDOM NATION

That is how, in a three thousand member church, there was no one with an unmet need. They couldn't just use the resources; if they did, they would be depleted in a matter of time. They had to use a system to trade and multiply what they had. Remember, they knew the parable of the talents that Jesus told them. He had taught them to use their talents to trade, invest, give for interest, or at least put it in a bank (Luke 19:11-27).

The Kingdom Family Bank is where God's people can keep or invest their money, instead of giving it to big corporations or the banks of this world. If God's people worldwide become a part of this bank, we will become the most powerful economic force on the earth.

> Every other religion and sect on the earth has a bank; Muslims, Catholics and Hindus have their own banks.

> I have written a book on *Kingdom Economy* that you may order from our website to study this.

5. Kingdom Education

The current education system under which we were all brought up was put in place, not to help the people, but to brain wash and program them to become slaves to a system for the rest of their lives. Actually, the education system that is out there was introduced by colonialism.

It is a trap that is set up to catch an individual who is created in the likeness and image of God, and who has been sent here to build God's kingdom, to condition them to be a copy and cause them to serve a system for a small amount of money every month, which we call a salary.

The goal of our current education system is to train a person to get a job in Babylon and then introduce them to a system that runs on debt. It allows them to buy houses, cars, and other gadgets they can't afford, and causes them to spend the rest of their lives paying for it all.

Consider the time you spend doing a job to make some money, and the majority, or all of that money, goes to pay for these things. How sad is it that we spend our precious life paying for some pieces of wood and metal?

A kingdom is a country, nation, or a territory that is ruled by a king. In the country where we were naturally born, we spent at least twelve years for our basic education. We were being trained to survive in the Babylonian system. When we are born again into God's kingdom, we need to be trained to fulfill our God-given purpose. That is why we need Kingdom Education. Kingdom Education is to train individuals to discover their God-given purpose.

Five Goals of Kingdom Education

1. The ultimate goal of Kingdom Education is to establish God's kingdom and will on the earth

2. Help a person discover their purpose, identity, calling, and gifts

3. Self-discovery

4. Managing and maximizing the resources (natural and spiritual) God gave us—Stewardship

5. Self-governance—By restoring their relationship with God as their Father

We need Kingdom Schools and Kingdom Universities in every nation. Right now, we have Kingdom Schools happening in more than ten countries. If you are interested in starting a Kingdom School, please contact us.

6. Kingdom Culture

We all grew up in different cultures. Every nation on earth has its own culture. We were brought up in the culture of the country of our natural birth. The way we think and live is based on that culture. Because we were trained from childhood, what we do and the way we think seems natural to us, and everything outside of it seems unreasonable or wrong.

Every culture has been infiltrated by demonic forces. A culture is made of belief systems, customs, language, arts, crafts, music, and superstitions. When we are spiritually born, we are born into a kingdom—the kingdom of God has its own culture.

I grew up in the Indian culture. In the olden days, according to the Indian culture, if a husband died prematurely, the blame was put on the wife. They believed he died because of the bad luck of the wife. According to their tradition, when they burned the husband's body, the wife was supposed to jump into the fire and end her life. That was a demonic custom and a superstition they used to practice.

When I came to the United States, I heard about Santa Clause and the Easter Bunny. Those are part of the culture and have nothing to do with the kingdom of God. After we are born again, each one of us needs to make a transition from the culture of our upbringing to the culture of the kingdom of God.

Sadly, most people don't make that transition. They continue to remain in the culture they were brought up in. Racism, the caste system, and tribalism are part of the cultures of this world. In the kingdom culture, there is no racism, caste system, or tribalism. We are all children of the same Father and citizens of the same kingdom.

Culture is the total sum of what we believe, the way we do things, and the way we think. Jesus's kingdom has its own culture, and He introduced that in the first sermon He preached. What we call the beatitudes in the Gospel of Matthew, is actually an introduction to His kingdom culture.

Matthew chapters 5-7 are the culture of Jesus's kingdom, or what I call the Kingdom Manifesto. There are several parables that Jesus shared to reveal the culture of His kingdom. The good Samaritan, the prodigal son, the unjust judge, the unforgiving servant, and many others, are there to reveal to us how life works and how we should think and live in God's kingdom.

Unfortunately, believers bring the culture of the country of their natural birth to the church, and that is why we still have racism, division, and colonialism in the world today. If people were treated equally in the church, it would become a safe haven for the people in the world, and they will flock to come to the church. We are supposed to be the light of this world.

7. Kingdom Government

I have already written two chapters about this, so I will not repeat it here, but please refer to those chapters to learn about Kingdom Government.

8. Kingdom Army

Every nation and kingdom has an army. The Kingdom Nation also has an army, but this army doesn't fight with natural weapons. The greatest weapon we have against our enemy is our humility and wisdom.

> For the weapons of our warfare *are* not carnal but mighty in God for pulling down strongholds, casting down arguments and every high thing that exalts itself against the

knowledge of God, bringing every thought into captivity to the obedience of Christ, and being ready to punish all disobedience when your obedience is fulfilled. (2 Corinthians 10:4-6)

Each citizen of the Kingdom Nation is a soldier. Whether we like it or not, everyone is in a battlefield, so we need to learn to fight. But the good news about this battle is that the victory is already won. This is the only battle on earth that you go into knowing the victory is already yours. It is because of what Jesus did on the cross to defeat our enemy.

You therefore must endure hardship as a good **soldier** of Jesus Christ. (2 Timothy 2:3)

It is important to create a mindset of victory to live this life. You're not fighting to win, but to enforce the victory that was already won by our King Jesus. Just knowing who you are in Christ and believing the victory Jesus has already won for us, sets the stage and models the attitude for how we face life and obstacles. This is very important. That is why the Bible says we need to "stand."

Most believers try to get victory for the battles they are facing, and they seldom prevail. If our heart and mind are not already set, then the fight gets harder. The Kingdom Nation army fights the following ways.

Prayer: Everyone is commanded and required to pray. Prayer is not telling God what to do. In religion, prayer is one-way communication. In the kingdom, prayer is a two-way conversation. It is communion with God.

Intercession: Intercession is not just praying for someone but standing in the gap for someone, as if you're that person. You get to experience what the other person is feeling and going through. It is a sacrifice that you are doing for someone that you love and care for, or it could be an assignment from God.

Warfare: There are different kinds of warfare in the kingdom. There is wrestling, as we read in Ephesians 6:12. There is prophetic preemptive warfare, which means seeing or knowing in the spirit what the enemy is planning to do and destroying it before he can manifest his schemes.

Deliverance: We all need to experience deliverance, and this is an ongoing process. It is deactivating, disconnecting, disassociating, and destroying every influence of the devil and his kingdom from our life, beginning with our bloodline, soul, conception, then DNA, birth, and birthright (Romans 7:6; Colossians 1:13; 1 Thessalonians 1:10).

Special Task Force: There are times when certain ambassadors need to be sent out on special missions to accomplish specific tasks for the King and the kingdom. These individuals will be highly trained and sensitive to the Holy Spirit to discern and see what both kingdoms are doing. These people should be "seers" in the spirit. This means they should have the capacity to see into the spirit realm.

9. Kingdom Media

Lucifer was anointed by God with a very unique anointing. Actually, the word used to describe his anointing is mentioned only once in the entire Bible. We see that word in Ezekiel 12:14.

That word means to imagine and create and spread quickly. Lucifer was in charge of God's kingdom economy, media, innovation, and manufacturing in relation to earth. That is why it is very hard for God's people to penetrate media, economy, innovation, manufacturing, and marketing—because they were his forte.

I would encourage you to read the book *The Gospel of the Kingdom* to find out where Lucifer was before he fell. He was not in heaven playing music or leading worship as we were told. He was a king, and he had a kingdom.

The enemy and his children can make something and spread it so quickly; they can market it worldwide and at lightning speed. Their news and ideas spread quickly. Though Lucifer fell, God did not take back his anointing. Though it got corrupted, it is still working for his advantage and to advance his kingdom.

That is why Jesus told us to be wise as serpents and innocent as doves. He wants us to study the wisdom God gave to the serpent, but when we use it, we need to be innocent as a dove. We cannot do things that are unrighteous and corrupt.

We need to take back that anointing from the enemy and use it for God's kingdom. God already blessed us to be fruitful, to multiply, and to fill the earth. We read about this in the first chapter of Genesis.

We need to use all available media platforms that are out there to advance the gospel of the kingdom. There is nothing wrong with using them. My only caution is, don't get addicted to them and spend the majority of your time playing games.

To be honest with you, Facebook played an important role in my life by connecting me with people from all across the globe for a kingdom purpose. The Kingdom School was birthed, and many major connections happened through Facebook. Especially during the locked-down season, it was a blessing to connect and advance the message of the kingdom to the nations of the world.

10. Kingdom Agriculture

In many parts of the world, people die because of a lack of food, while others die because of food or consuming the wrong kind of food.

Knowing the importance of what we eat, God had to take the initiative in the book of Genesis to show us what is good by coming down and planting a garden.

Food is a serious business. Believe it or not, sin and every form of evil we see came into the world today just because the first Adam chose to eat the wrong fruit. Mankind eating the wrong food even cost the life of the only begotten Son of God. It's hard to comprehend.

Knowing the importance of what we eat and its consequences, the enemy took over the entire production and marketing of the food industry in every nation. He who controls the food industry controls the quality and longevity of our life.

Eating the wrong kind of food has the capacity to influence us spiritually, emotionally, and physically. The opposite is true as well. It is important that we eat food with a gladness of heart. If we eat it worrying or sad, it affects our digestion and the absorption of nutrients into our bloodstream.

Each family should have a garden, just like the first family, Adam and Eve, had a garden to manage. God was showing an example for every other family to follow. We really need to filter and sensor what goes into our mouth.

The enemy and his kingdom (the wicked) has a vested interest in the agriculture of every nation. Kingdom citizens need to take it back from the enemy. The wicked are not trying to help us; they are trying to steal, kill, and destroy. They want to steal what God gave to us, kill the life of God in us, and eventually, destroy us. He cannot destroy us if he cannot first steal what God gave to us. While destroying us, they want to make money.

The goal of the majority of this world's food production is to extort money from us. The goal of everything the wicked does is to monetize their products and services. That's the purpose of drug trafficking also. They don't care about the youth or their future. They want to destroy them and make some money while doing it.

When we do Kingdom Agriculture, we must make sure the seeds we use are not genetically modified. We need to find the original seeds and plants that God started and preserve them for generations to come. The purpose of Kingdom Agriculture shouldn't be to make money; the purpose should be the health and well-being of God's people.

We have started a small scale farming program in different countries. It is in its inception stage. We are dreaming to recapture God's idea of food production and consumption. We need kingdom universities that are just focused on agriculture and food production. Every school on this earth needs to include a curriculum on gardening and kingdom farming as part of their education.

The focus of a kingdom nation should be its own food production, processing, and distribution system that is separated from this world.

11. Kingdom Industries

The first introduction and revelation of God we see in the Bible is as the Creator. In the beginning, God *created* the heavens and the earth (Genesis 1:1). We are created in the image and likeness of God. That means we are created to function as He functions. We are supposed to produce or make by manifesting the creativity of God. That is one of the ways we manifest the image and likeness of God.

Unfortunately, the church became the most consuming agency on the earth. We use everything the world produces and then come to church and sing *This World is Not My Home*. In most places, if the people in the world stop producing food and other necessities,

Christians would die of starvation or would be forced to go back to a primitive lifestyle.

We need kingdom Industries. We need to start producing *everything* we need, from a pencil to an airplane. We need to bring quality and useful products to the market. We live in a world where everything is duplicated. In some parts of the world, every product they buy from the markets are duplicates. That shouldn't be so.

We have two groups of people: producers and consumers. Producers make decisions for the consumers. They have a strong influence over them. God doesn't make cars and airplanes. He created the raw materials and gave us the imagination and creativity to produce what we need.

We have been trained to look for a miracle or for someone to give us something for free. Looking for a miracle is the sign that we are still in our wilderness journey and have not reached the place of our destiny (promised land) yet.

When we are in the wilderness, God *fights for us* and *provides for us*. When we reach the promised land, the situation changes. There God wants to *fight through* us and *work through* us. There is a huge difference between how God relates with us and works with us in both places. In the promised land, God wants us to partner with Him in accomplishing His will.

In the promised land, God wants us to plant and produce things. He promised to bless the works of our hands. If we don't do anything, there is nothing for Him to bless. The church has not entered into the promised land season yet because we were taught that the promised land is heaven. So the majority spend their entire life wandering in the wilderness without fulfilling their destiny. The people of Israel spent only forty years in the wilderness and we feel bad for them, but the church has been in the wilderness for over two thousand years.

The first miracle Jesus did was turn water into wine. For Him to turn the water into wine, He first told the people to fill the water jars with water. Jesus was not going to do that. With the establishment of the Kingdom Nation comes the responsibility of producing and manufacturing what we need. A nation cannot survive without the necessary survival products.

12. Kingdom Healthcare

We need to take care of our health and body. When we lose our body, we become illegal on the earth. We are only useful to God and his kingdom while we are on the earth. Being on the earth is not a mistake or part of the curse.

When I travel in India, I see hospitals and medical clinics all over the place. Hospitals are popping up everywhere like gas (petrol) stations. The food industry causes the people to become sick, and hospitals take advantage of it.

God never wanted us to be treated with medicine that we see in hospitals. He wanted food to be our medicine. God included everything our body needs to live healthy, in plants, herbs, and seeds. Not only to live healthy, but if something goes wrong with our body, everything our body needs is in nature.

The current healthcare system exploits people and runs on making money. This must change. We need to start Kingdom Healthcare centers across the globe. There are three main ingredients to Kingdom Healthcare: using things that are natural for our food and well-being, prioritizing mental health, and cultivating healthy relationships. I believe that if we follow these three principles, we can evade almost all sicknesses and diseases.

THE BIRTHING OF A KINGDOM NATION

When we manifest these twelve components of the kingdom in the nations of our world, transformation will begin to happen. Each of us carries a component of the kingdom inside of us. That is the kingdom we are supposed to see when we are born again.

May the Lord help us to implement what is written in this book. The revelation in this book is only a nutshell of the vision and the plan God has for His Kingdom Nation. This is only a seed, and from this, by the help of the Holy Spirit, let us build God's nation in partnership with Him and with one another. Amen.

We encourage you to become a part of this Kingdom Nation by becoming a citizen of it. There are many benefits. You were not created to live in a corner of this world and die unnoticed. The Lord wants you to be a part of His kingdom. You will find the tribe that you belong to. Go to www.RegnoEthnos.com to find outmore information on how to become a citizen of God's Kingdom Nation.

I pray that what you read and learned from this book, you will keep undefiled. What you read is part of the heart of our heavenly Father. May the Lord keep this undefiled from the Babylonian and Egyptian systems and spirits. Please do not mix this with religion or use this to build something of your own. May generations to come benefit from this. Let them come and drink from the River of Life and eat from the Tree of Life.

> Now if anyone builds on this foundation *with* gold, silver, precious stones, wood, hay, straw, each one's work will become clear; for the Day will declare it, because it will be revealed by fire; and the fire will test each one's work, of what sort it is. If anyone's work which he has built on *it* endures, he will receive a reward. If anyone's work is burned, he will

suffer loss; but he himself will be saved, yet so as through fire. (1 Corinthians 3:12-15)

More Books & Resources

DISCIPLING NATIONS SERIES

Kingdom Mandate (for any donation)
Discovering the Lost Kingdom (Volume 1) $14.00
Purpose, Calling, and Gifts (Volume 2) $15.00
God's Original Design (Volume 3) $20.00
Seeing, Entering, and Manifesting the Kingdom of God (Volume 4)$20.00
The Ekklesia (Volume 5) $30.00
The Gospel of the Kingdom (Volume 6) $20.00
Power and Authority of the Church (Volume 7) $15.00
Kingdom Family (Volume 8) $15.00
The Birthing of a kingdom nation (Volume 9) $20.00
What happened to God (Volume10) $20.00
7 Dimensions and Operations of the Kingdom of God (Volume 11)$15.00
Kingdom Economy (Volume 12) $15.00
Kingdom Government (Volume 13) $15.00
Releasing Kings and Queens to their Original Intent (Volume 14) $10.00
Kingdom Secrets to Restoring Nations Back to God (Volume 15) $20.00

KINGDOM LIVING SERIES

The Three Most Important Decisions of Your Life $15.00
Keys to Passing Your Spiritual Tests $15.00
Recognizing God's Timing for Your Life $12.00
Overcoming the Spirit of Poverty $10.00
Seven Kinds of Believers $10.00
7 Dimensions of God's Glory $5.00
7 Dimensions of God's Grace $10.00
7 Kinds of Faith $7.00

KINGDOM BOOKS FOR KIDS

Genesis 126 Three Volume Book set for boys $25.00

TO PLACE AN ORDER:
www.TheKingdomNetwork.org
Phone: 1-800-558-5020
Email: info@TheKingdomNetwork.org

Are you struggling to discover your **PURPOSE ?**
You are not supposed to fit in but stand out !

Sign up today for the upcoming
FREE Online Kingdom Course

DISCOVERING

THE LOST KINGDOM

In this course you'll DISCOVER:

>> Your true identity and purpose
>> What God is doing on the earth and how you can partner with Him in it
>> Why God created the earth and put us on this planet
  And much more ...

Why are people becoming more and more disinterested in **church and religion** globally?
Join the course, and discover
what your soul has been searching for all along.

FREE BOOK AND STUDY GUIDE

other courses available
>> DISCOVERING PURPOSE, CALLING AND GIFTS
>> SEEING, ENTERING AND MANIFESTING THE KINGDOM
>> GOD'S ORIGINAL DESIGN | FEBRUARY 2024
>> The Ekklesia
>> The Next move of GOD
   And more ...

Register Now @ **www.TheKingdomUniversity.org**

www.ingramcontent.com/pod-product-compliance
Lightning Source LLC
Chambersburg PA
CBHW070134080526
44586CB00015B/1696